What is mentionable is manageable—a creativity journal

Compassionately understanding one's soul in the weird new normal of 2020

What is mentionable is manageable—a creativity journal

Compassionately understanding one's soul in the weird new normal of 2020

Carolyn Klassen

ISBN: 978-1-7772256-2-9

To the medical teams that heal us,
To the researchers that will find us a way out of this.
To the essential staff that serve us,
We extend our gratitude.
Words are not enough to show you how much we appreciate you.

Contents

ACKNOWLEDGMENTS X

INTRODUCTION XII

MISCREANT MONSTER AND MAGI 1

WE ARE ALL A LITTLE FRAGILE THESE DAYS 3

PANDEMICS REMIND US OF OUR VULNERABILITY 5

THE LAST NORMAL DAY 8

THE NEW NORMAL 11

ALL BEHAVIOR IS COMMUNICATION 14

PERMISSION TO NOT BE GOOD AT THIS 17

NOBODY KNOWS HOW TO DO A PANDEMIC 22

STANDARD TRANSMISSIONS: RPM'S 27

STRESS IS EXHAUSTING 31

STRESSIN' ABOUT THE STRESS 34

ANGER, BLAME AND JUDGEMENT 38

OTHER PROBLEMS CONTINUE 41

WHAT WAS TRUE BEFORE CONTINUES TO BE TRUE OR EVEN TRUER 43

GRIEF 45

SECOND BEST HAS GOTTEN OLD 50

THE TIME OF PANDEMIC AS TRAUMA 52

GROUNDING 55

RISK AVERSE AND RISK ACCEPTANT—YOURS, MINE, OURS 58

THIS MATH DOESN'T WORK FOR PARENTS 62

BOUNDARIES 65

SKIN HUNGER 68

DISCONNECTION IS PAINFUL AND CONNECTION IS HEALING 71

THE PANDEMIC AS MAGI—WISDOM GIVER 75

COMPOSTING HEARTBREAK 78

REDEMPTIVE SUFFERING   82

GRATITUDE   87

EXISTENTIAL DISCOVERY   92

GRACE   95

EPILOGUE   99

ABOUT THE AUTHOR   101

Acknowledgments

This is the part of the book where an author thanks all the people who provided mentoring and ideas and inspired them.

Book acknowledgements are all about thanking the ones who made a **book** possible. This book's acknowledgements are for the people who are making **life** possible. Thank you to the nurses and doctors and allied health staff like respiratory therapists, social workers, housekeeping and dietary services who are saving lives in the hospital. Thank you to the guy at the gas pump, and the woman who wipes my cart at Coop before I get my groceries, the pharmacy technician at the drugstore for working through a pandemic to give us the services that keep us going. Thank you to all the workers who spend time first thing in the morning and throughout the day wiping things down places of business to increase safety. Thank you to the delivery person who dropped off the food from the restaurant we ordered, and to those who prepared the food. Thank you to the men and women who wear masks and maintain social distancing, to the people who sit at home even though they are bored and would rather go outside, to the ones who are worried about income and rent and all the rest of it but wait. Thank you to the researcher who are working around the clock for a way out of this. Thank you to the innovators who are creating ways to move us forward even under adverse circumstances—your creativity inspired this book.

You are all my heroes. You keep us alive.

I am grateful

creativity *will* be beautiful, because it is yours.

Can you extend me the same grace? I've put together this book because I believe we need it. I could spend more time proofing it for errors, and tweaking phrases—but I wanted it to be available now. You see my efforts—imperfect but well intentioned. Know that each little error is a sign of my humanity. ☺

Use this book in whatever way it works for you! There will be some who have to put the book down—you just need to focus on breathing and getting through the day. This might not be the right season to take yourself to the big feelings and explore them. You might just need to focus on the next right thing—shower, feed the kids, lunchtime, etc. If that's where you're at, can you give yourself permission to say, "Not right now"? Others of you will find some chapters appealing and others might feel, "too much". Do this when and how it feels right.

Do one chapter a day—or week, in order, out of order, skip a chapter—have this book serve you in whatever way is meaningful. Please don't rush through it—the creative prompts are meant to savor and ponder. Likely you can do it this month and you'll get one set of answers. Next month, you can start all over again and your answers will shift and layer and deepen.

The links in this book were active as of the date of publication.

Introduction

Tom Hanks was the first person I knew to get the virus when he announced that he and his wife, Rita Wilson, contracted it while in Australia. All of a sudden, what seemed like an exotic, far away illness seemed much closer—though, at that moment, still on the other side of the world.

The pandemic has since taken over the world in 2020. It has impacted the global community's health and economic stability, infecting millions and killing over a quarter of million people at the time of this writing. We are washing hands, worrying, social distancing and learning how to make bread at a pace we couldn't have imagined only a couple of months ago.

Tom Hanks played Mr. Rogers in *A Beautiful Day in the Neighborhood*[1], a beautiful film released last year. I loved that movie for so many reasons, but not least of which was this: it gave me a key message on an important day. I had gone to see it on my husband's late wife's birthday. I went out that evening on my own, to give my husband an opportunity to spend time with his family remembering his first love. He had spent the day watching videos of his young family when she was alive and vibrant. He remembered her before the surgeries, the chemo and the radiation took so much from her.

The key message I took away from the movie was this, a lesson Mr. Roger's gave to a journalist who was struggling with bitterness in his life:

Anything that's human is mentionable and anything that is mentionable can be more manageable. When we can talk about our feelings, they become less overwhelming, less upsetting, and less scary.

The movie's message confirmed the importance of giving him space to grieve his late wife, and reminded me all over again about how fantastic this husband of mine is.

As a therapist, I definitely find this idea of "the mentionable becomes manageable" to be true in my work with clients. And thus, this book. We are going to look at various ways in which the pandemic is affecting our world—and then I'm going to invite you to

---

[1] "A Beautiful Day in the Neighborhood." *IMDb*, IMDb.com, 22 Nov. 2019, www.imdb.com/title/tt3224458/.

name how it is affecting *you*.

If you feel it, you can heal it.

It's not as simple as that, but there is truth to it. This pandemic is creating big feelings, huge losses, and incredible change—processing it will be good for you.

I'll give you several prompts to use as fodder. Grab something with which to be creative. This isn't about *good* or *bad* art or writing—it's about giving yourself permission to explore your inner world in a way that feels like you can express yourself. Perhaps a journal and a pen. If you prefer pictures, grab color pencils. If you like to journal electronically, create a blank page and put your fingers on the keyboard ready to type. I'll invite you to explore your own COVID-19 experience through whatever means you like:

- Write poetry or lists or paragraphs
- Draw or paint words or pictures or abstracts
- Cut pictures from magazines, or take photos with your phone or make a quilt
- Use these at the dinner table and share your responses verbally. Record them. Or not.

In short, use this book as a way to explore and express yourself during this time. Use the creative prompts as a springboard to launch your own creative ideas to explore. I invite you to share your work using with #MentionableisManageable so that we can enjoy each other's work. You will further another's move through this pandemic with the gift of your work!

As you can process our feelings, you can move through them.

As you can name the hard stuff, you get to make decisions about how you hold it, rather than have it hold you as hostage.

As you name what is really happening inside of you, you have opportunity to make decisions about what to do with big feelings that, without acknowledgement, will make your decisions for you!

Let this book become a personal memoir of sorts. As you write your thoughts, feelings, experiences and actions in this book, it will capture important parts of you during this time. It will be a way to capture these unprecedented times so that you have an ability to look back on them in the future.

Don't be too fussy about the product. Avoid self-judgment—or give yourself to feel it, and move through it. When you are tempted to say, "I'm not a good writer. I can't draw good enough," can you kindly support yourself? The beauty is in the expression. Your

Miscreant Monster and Magi

COVID-19 is impacting our entire world in powerful ways. Lockdowns, quarantines, stay-at-home orders, hand sanitizer, social distancing, ventilators. Words that rarely entered our world now have common usage.

I have been thinking about COVID-19 as affecting our lives in 3 main ways:

MISCREANT: A miscreant is one who behaves criminally or viciously. The virus steals lives. It attacks the lungs. It can hoodwink a person because they think they are getting better and then their condition nosedives. The virus can lurk silently amongst many people unawares and then it attacks. It often attacks the vulnerable, but sometimes it has victory over the strong and healthy.

MONSTER: Remember those black and white monster movies. Ominous music, pounding footsteps that shook the camera, and eerie shadows. The thought that the monster was around was just as bad as dealing with the monster. Chaos, people running and hiding, trying to get away. The monster attacked people's spirits, minds and hearts as they began to relate to each other from a place of fear. Their daily lives changed as they sought to avoid it. For some, it brought out the ugly. Others were courageously heroic. But all were impacted as they sought to avoid the monster.

COVID-19 is affecting all of us, even as we might not have the disease.

Unemployment, financial distress, homeschooling, shops closed, planes grounded, travel bans in place, stay at home orders, quarantines. The list goes on and on.

MAGI: Magi are known to be wisdom givers, to look beyond the obvious to see more. The wise men who visited Jesus in Bethlehem came, bearing gifts that had prophetic value.
I believe that times of difficulty and darkness can be times of growth and learning. Please don't see this as simplistic as, "COVID-19 has come to the world to teach us a lesson." Or "COVID-19 has come to the world as punishment". Absolutely not.

I don't think the COVID-19 is a good gift in itself. I will never be grateful for the COVID-19 virus. However, I do believe that as we pay attention to the world and the people in it, to ourselves in our inner being—we can receive gifts from this time. Some of the wisdom and some of the gifts may be apparent now. The deeper and more profound gifts will only develop with the passage of time. I like to be curious about the ability of COVID-19 being a *magus* (singular form of the plural *magi*).

Creative Prompts

If you imagine COVID-19 as a miscreant—what does he (or maybe, to you COVID-19 is a she or an it?) look like? What sort of clothes does this miscreant wear? What does he smell like? What sort of music does he listen to? What food does he likes? What is his cocktail? Be playful.

If you imagine COVID-19 as a monster—what shape does he/she/it take? What is the texture and color of his skin/hair? How large is the monster? What sound does he make? What is his diet? When and where does he come out?

If you imagine COVID-19 as magus—what sort of animal does he/she/it ride to enter your life? What do the gifts look like? What sort of expression does the magi wear? Where does the magi come from? What else does the magi want you to know about him/her/itself? This is a chance to personify COVID-19. You can't do it wrong. Your creations will say something important. You might want to post on social media with the hashtag #MentionableisManageable. It will allow us to share with each other!

We are all a little fragile these days

I'm feeling a little fragile these days. I suspect you too

I need more sleep than usual. I can be a little irritable.

I crave carbs like I crave breathing. I determine to be more deliberate about eating, and to have a better day—and round about 8:00 pm, it falls apart and I hunt down salty and sweet snacks like one of those shoppers in sale of the ultimate deal on Black Friday.

I can wake up in the morning ready to attack my day, with a list of things to do and a plan on how I will do them.

And occasionally, I can pull it off. That feels great.

Sometimes, I get half of it done.

Some days, well, some days, I don't.

I'm reading and thinking and praying. I'm trying to be mindful. I'm trying to get exercise. I listen to books because I know this relaxes me.

I know what is good for me. But my ability to translate that into solid dependable behaviour right now is shaky at best.

We had a late spring here in the heart of Canada. A couple of times it was warm—

pleasant even. And several times, it turned back to winter, and big soft fluffy flakes came down. When the weather turns to winter like this even for 45 minutes, I get ridiculously discouraged. I can't find beauty in the flakes—only discouragement.

My ability to live into knowing that spring always come disappears out of my mind like I'm a goldfish with a 10 second attention span.

I had a list of phone calls to make—8 of them. To total strangers. Not my thing—but I can do hard things. And on the scale of difficult, a phone call to stranger is normally fairly low on the *hard scale*. It felt like it took more than I had in me to make them. It took me almost 2 weeks to finish this simple job. I felt small and the task felt too big.

I watch television and there are beautiful commercials of front-line workers in slow motion, cheering from balconies, empty stadiums, and grocery store workers wearing masks, and tears develop. I haven't cried at commercials since my hormones were out of whack right after I had a baby.

I'm drawn to those virtual choirs on YouTube like watching them will save my life. Because in that moment, they do.

It's that fragility, I think.

I'm ok—mostly. The uncertainty of the timeline of this virus is daunting. Having loved ones work on the frontline is unnerving. It's disconcerting to hear of shortages of medical supplies and equipment. It's disheartening to hear of people who don't feel like their boss is keeping them safe.

We are all a little tender right now.

It's not easy to feel fragile, is it?

Creative prompts:

When is/are the moment(s) you felt most fragile?

What do you do when you feel fragile?

What picture/image depicts what your fragility looks/feels like?

Who else in your world do you imagine is fragile? What gives you this suspicion? How is their fragility different than yours?

Pandemics remind us of our vulnerability

We had a rough start to the morning, the not-so-little one and I back in March. First day of home schooling. I had hopes and expectations, wanted to establish a start to some healthy routines, so I got on his case. The internet said routines were important for children—it was good for them. In other words, good parents establish structure. Dang it, I was going to do the good parent thing.

Funny enough, he didn't see my efforts as well intentioned, and told me so. Then, I got all up in his grill about it. He didn't like that either—and let me know. We were glaring at each other and using a volume that rarely is heard in our house.

I'm not a yeller. I'm just not. But I was that day. I lost it in a way that was very uncharacteristic of me.

I backed off first and let him know we'd pick this up later. (Sometimes, even when I'm in the middle of the ugly, I know enough to spare others the worst of it.) I took that ugly to my workstation.

It took about 45 minutes at my computer for me to calm down to see that the uncertainty of this pulled me into wanting to nail something down. Brené Brown defines vulnerability[2] as risk, uncertainty and emotional exposure.

That pretty much describes the definition of what a pandemic feels like to a soul, doesn't it?

I got all controll-y because life suddenly seemed so very out of control. I wanted to make *something* certain because all of life has suddenly gotten so dang vulnerable. I needed him to have a routine so I would be better. I needed him to be successful at homeschooling under my tutelage because I would feel a little less vulnerable.

Feel is the operative word here. I wouldn't have actually been any less vulnerable, because there is no outrunning the global vulnerability that we have all been plunged into with COVID-19. In fact, even before the virus there was no outrunning vulnerability. Letting our kids out of the door to go to school, saying, "I love you" for the first time, asking him out for date, asking her for a promotion, going on a trip to a new destination, going to the doctor. It's all vulnerable. But we forget that sometimes—and the virus has reminded us all that certainty was always an illusion.

That morning, I got a little teary sitting there at my computer. I realized that my efforts to be a good parent had made me be a lousy parent. My effort to control the situation—to manage him—ended disastrously. We do that when we're stressed sometimes—don't we? Make it worse because we get wound so tight trying to do it well.

I needed to go apologize. Routines and patterns are important to establish—but not with a sledgehammer when we are all a little eggshell-ish.

We're all a little on edge. The solid ground of "normal life" seems a fiction now. Strange routines. Unknown timelines. Fractured political divides that make the differences more important than the disease. We feel the vulnerability frequently through the day, every day. Before COVID-19 many of us could go weeks without being aware of it, until something like a flat tire—or a car accident—reminded us that certitude is something elusive.

We are all a little fragile. Remind yourself to take deep breaths. What happens when you try to make life certain, perfect, safe, controllable and predictable? It doesn't work. It never did.

Take a step back when you feel some sharpness in your tone. Wait until you have a chance to be present and kind with yourself. We take care of others gently as we are first

---

[2] Brown, Brene. *Daring Greatly: How the Courage to Be Vulnerable Transforms the Way We Live, Love, Parent and Lead.* Penguin, 2012.

gentle with ourselves.

That morning was a rough start. It was a powerful reminder of how the effort to control, perfect and plan creeps into my life and bites someone I care about in the butt.

Hey, consider this a gentle reminder to be aware of when vulnerability is pulling you out of the best of you into a control freak. As you can recognize what you are doing, you can choose to embrace the vulnerability. You can gently feel the tightening that comes with feeling vulnerable—and then release and loosen into the truth that vulnerability will be there regardless of the efforts you make.

Creative prompts:

When have been some "pandemic moments" where you have felt particularly vulnerable? What are the snapshot moments that capture the risk and emotional exposure of this time?

What does vulnerability look like? What does it smell and taste like?

Write a letter to this sense of vulnerability in your life. Let Vulnerability know what it is like to live with. Can you express your reluctance to have it in your life, but also the moments that gave you something beautiful?

The last normal day

The last normal day was Thursday, March 12 where I live. That was *my* last normal day. The day before, on March 11, we heard the NBA was on hold and Tom Hanks had been infected with COVID-19. Those felt a wee bit closer to home, but still very much not in my area. COVID-19 didn't affect me.

March 12 was a day I delivered a workshop to a government department. About 40 people had registered, but the group was much smaller because some were pulled into meetings about how the virus was affecting their department's mission. The smaller group or the virus weren't the issue that morning—technical problems were. The night before the technicians had upgraded the audiovisual system and so we couldn't get the screen and the speakers to work in their boardroom.

We had a great day talking about issues of fear and vulnerability and courage. We spoke about taking risks and being brave. As we spoke about these matters, I asked them how these topics intersected with their lives. We had engaged conversation about their lives—their struggles and fears—and the virus didn't come up. Not once.

I dashed home from the workshop because I had 25 athletes, coaches and support staff coming to my home for supper that night. They had flown in for the University Sports National Volleyball Championship. I was looking forward to visiting with son's friends and giving them a good feed the day before the last tournament of the year—for some the last one in their university career. Students in dorm crave a great meal. They came into the 8-team tournament ranked first and would be playing on March 13th against the home team. It was a sell-out, standing room only crowd in the university center. My son had played for the team the past 5 years. The home team's coach was retiring after a stellar career and it was going to be an incredible night.

Moments before they arrived, we discovered conference organizers would not allow fans into the gym the next night. They would play the national tournament without an audience. Texts were flying back and forth as we figured out alternate plans to watch together at a nearby restaurant. While the athletes were consuming enormous amounts of pasta, they shared stories about how some provinces were extending their spring break to 3 weeks.

It all seemed so strange and fantastical. Surely it was an overreaction? Maybe they wouldn't actually follow through? Denial is a real thing.

The athletes left to go back to their hotel. Shortly after they arrived, they received notice the entire tournament was cancelled.

They flew home the next morning without playing a game.

By the end of the day, another son's high school put out notice that they were anticipating closing by mid-week the following week—for just a few weeks.

Around our house, life went from normal to weird in a day and a half.

When I look back on it now, I wonder, "If I had known in early March that life was about to change so drastically, and so much of my 'normal life' would be erased, what would I have done? How would I have spent my evenings? What would I have wanted to do one last time before it was no longer allowed under the new guidelines?"

Creative Prompts:

Think about your last normal day: What happened? What did you do? What were the first things that suggested to you that your life was about to undergo a major shift? It might be meaningful to record that last normal day while it is still relatively fresh in your mind.

Was it surreal? Did it feel like it was really happening? When were the moments it started to *sink in?*

Have a little creative fun: If you had known the last 7 days before the stay-at-home orders came, before planes stopped flying and restaurants closed that it was coming, how would you have chosen to spend those days? What would you have done? Where would you have wanted to go? Who would you have wanted to visit one last time before everyone went home to stay?

The new normal

The Junior in my house is wrapping his head around *school cancelled indefinitely* for the year. We all are. We had initially hoped that this would all blow over in a couple of weeks.

Reality set in. This would be a couple of months, then likely a couple of seasons. Over time, it became apparent it could possibly be a couple of years before the virus ceases to be a threat. It became time to get serious about planning what life looks like now that we are realizing this is a "new normal".

It was hard to imagine routine not resuming after Spring Break. We were surprised by, but ready to roll with the idea of things stopping for several weeks. We knew it could be longer, but it was hard to wrap our heads around it. It's here now.

The school emptied his locker, putting the contents in a garbage bag. We drove up to the school at our slotted time and popped open the trunk while staying in the vehicle. They put the garbage bag in the trunk, and slammed the trunk closed.

And we drove away from the school for the last time this year. And we don't know what the next school year holds.

I couldn't have imagined the world we now live in:

- temperatures being taken before entering an office,

- spaced out designated spaces for people to wait,

- cotton swab sticks to press the debit machines,

- wiping surfaces between each customer

- masks on staff in retail services

- and predictions of children being expected to stay at their desks all day without moving

With vaccines taking months to develop, and still no effective known therapeutics, we realize we're settling into the long haul of virus containment.

We have to figure out how to make fluctuating levels of physical distancing sustainable. Our world is smaller and will be for the unknown future. There are empty spaces on the grocery store shelves and lineups to patiently wait to enter the store. We are learning how to be in the same space as the rest of our family all day and every evening. Working from home for many is now a reality. Borders closed, air travel down—no known timelines for when this will reverse.

What would have seemed impossible just months ago is now our life. Our new life.

This is my first pandemic. Yours too. We are each starting to get to know ourselves in this new normal:

- How we cope with more hours at home than ever before.

- What we miss, and how we compensate.

- What are surprising things we now enjoy that we didn't expect.

- What is especially hard in ways that others can't understand.

- The big feelings we are experiencing that surprise us

- What others say or do that are just what we need

- What others say or do that grate on our last nerves

This is a new space for us to be in. When you're in a new country on vacation or on a week-long course, you can just "make do". You can bring crackers from home if you don't like the food. But when you move to a new country for a whole degree's worth of schooling or a three-year work term, it's important to figure out how to:

- settle in and have it become home

- find out what works and what doesn't

- learn how to belong in a new setting

- how to feel at home in this new and strange place, because it's going to be a while.

It's time to settle in and make the *new normal* feel like home.

Creative Prompts:

What have you learned about yourself—your preferences, your interests—during this time of COVID-19 living? What has surprised you? What do you find especially difficult?

Develop an "operating manual" that would outline to others about your current operating system. Write down ways in which you notice you value encouragement and support. What are your warning systems that something isn't going well? What is upsetting to the "COVID-19 version of you"? Imagine this manual as a tool that would teach others about what you have learned about how you move about in this "new normal". What have you discovered about yourself in the time since COVID-19 has so significantly impacted your world?

All Behavior is Communication

One of my colleagues used to work in a group home with disabled adults, some of whom were nonverbal. Their disabilities didn't allow for speech. She and I were talking one day about how to communicate with someone who couldn't speak. She said simply: "All behavior is a form of communication." Their approach as staff was to notice what the residents were doing and then be curious about what that behavior was saying.

It is fun for all of us to witness behaviors that communicate joy, contentment, and peace. But it takes a deep breath and some patience to notice what is being communicated when tears, stomping, flailing, and loud calls are expressed. It's tempting to just shut "problem" behaviors down without exploring what those behaviors are trying to say.

The group home staff might learn that one resident expressed he was hungry one way, while another one might do it with a whole other strategy. The staff had trained themselves to focus beyond the immediate inconvenience of the yelling or arms swinging to understand what these people were saying with these behaviors—were they tired, in pain, frustrated or overwhelmed?

In her mind, there were no "problem behaviors" amongst these folks. When a resident lashed out, rather than judging the behavior as "wrong", they got curious: "What is this communicating?"

They didn't try to shut down the behavior, even if—especially if—it was a "problem behavior". They sought to understand what that behavior was saying to enable the staff to address the underlying issue. The behavior could change when it didn't need to communicate the same message.

***

We think of babies like that too. We might see a niece or a nephew starting to cry, and the parent will say: "Just a minute, I have a diaper I need to change." Later the baby is crying again, and the parent understands that the child now needs a snack, or some quiet time away from people, or a nap. The parent has learned what unique sorts of crying are trying to signal. Telling a baby to stop crying doesn't work—nor would you want it to work.

***

In this age of COVID-19, you might notice yourself doing things that are different. Maybe some things you don't like. Things like:

- Eating more of certain kinds of food

- Eating more at certain times of day

- Feeling irritated and yelling at people

- Drinking alcohol more often, earlier in the day, or greater amounts

- Binge watching television series or movies—maybe certain kinds of shows

- Endlessly watching the news cycle, flipping from one network to another

- Scrolling through social media apps at length

***

Here's the thing: when you notice yourself engaging in a new behavior or changing your behavior, there will be a temptation to scold yourself. Judging oneself for "too much" or "not enough" of something is so easy to do.

What is more challenging, and I think, so much more adaptive, is to slow down and wonder:

- "What is this about?"

- "What is my behavior trying to communicate?"

- "What am I being asked to pay attention to inside of me?"

Creative prompts:

What atypical behaviors different from pre-COVID-19 life are you noticing now?

What do you imagine (or know) these behaviors are communicating?

If I am aware of the underlying message of what these behaviors are communicating, how does that change how I relate to myself? To those behaviors? What might I want to do to address the underlying messages in the most compassionate way possible?

Permission to not be good at this

I first discovered the power of the permission slip years ago when my oldest son, Adam, was in Grade 1.

He and his little brother were the absolutely most adorable blonde-haired kids. We let their hair grow longer in the winter, "bowl cut" style. We then buzzed it short with a hair trimmer for the summer when they played outside so often. I loved the look—they look at pictures of themselves when they were little and roll their eyes that I could have let them look like this.

In the spring, it was time to shear the children's heads. In the joyful chaos that was our household, the littlest one ran by first—and I swooped him up for his spring buzz-cut. I put the shaver attachment on "number 2", ensuring a short buzz, but with enough hair left that they looked adorable. Then, I pulled the shaver attachment off to neatly trim around the bottom at his neck and around his ears. I worked quickly, because little boys have a limited ability to sit still. Then, after he's done, he hops off the chair, and I call the older one over.

I'm in the hair shaving zone. I'm working well—in the groove. Ready to get the job done.

Now, Adam hops up onto the chair. I start with a strip going from the front at his hairline towards the back of his head—just off center of his head on the left side. I get about 4 or 5 inches along when I notice that he is reacting in pain, which is unusual. There is also more drag on the shaver than usual, too.

And that is when I notice I have not put the shaver attachment back on.

I'm not shaving his hair short. I'm shaving his hair gone.

Bald.

I stopped the moment I realized my error. But now he's got a stripe, 2 inches wide of pink tender scalp in between the rest of his head which still had the beautiful long, fine hair of winter. I looked with horror at what I'd done.

He asked for a mirror, and he felt the smooth strip of skin. And he began to cry. Hard.

I started to cry hard, too.

We were both weeping, realizing there was no way to fix this.

In the moment of a hard time, sometimes a person can catastrophize. We both catastrophized in that moment, neither of us could remember that hair grows back, all we could contemplate was the *terrible now*.

I sent him off to breathe and wash his face—mostly so I could do the same. I needed to collect myself.

After a time of sorrow for both of us, I allowed him to contemplate the best options I could think of, to make it "least worst" (there were no good options here):

1. I could shave his entire head bald so it matched and while he would be hairless, and then it would grow in evenly.

2. I could shave the rest of his head on the number 2 attachment, so that there was one smooth strip amongst the stubble, and it would look a little odd, but we would buzz him again in a couple of weeks to make it uniform.

Bless his little 6-year-old heart, he chose option

3: **The comb over.**

Evidently, he had seen the style at church with men covering their bald pate with the side hair and he was impressed.

So, we put in some hair product and tested out his choice.

It actually worked fairly effectively, as long as he sat perfectly still.

In other words, it didn't work.

We figured out a better solution: a ball cap. When he had the hat on, and the *comb over* gelled into place, he looked great.

The relief didn't last. However, he wailed again when he remembered that hats were forbidden in his school in the classroom, and that night was a school night. He had to show up for class the next day.

The next morning, he headed off to school with his front pockets full:

1. He had a note for his teacher. I explained the dilemma and asked for

mercy. I asked for permission for him to keep his cap on during the class.

2. He had several notes in his pocket that I had handwritten for him. They all said the same thing. Something like:

You might be tempted to make fun of me because of my hair today. However, it was my mom that is responsible, and so if you are going to make fun of anybody, it should be her. Her name is Carolyn and her number is xxx-xxxx. She would be happy to take your call.

The next day, as he got off the school bus, having managed a full day at school with a bald strip on his head, he fairly skipped and hopped off the bus.

I was not expecting that.

I asked him what happened. He said the after he handed the teacher the note, not only was he allowed to keep his cap on during the day, apparently the teacher had used this as a teachable moment. The entire class had gathered at her feet, as Adam stood beside her. She had reminded the students how sometimes things went wrong in everybody's life. It is at those moments that people need understanding and compassion. She let them know that day it was their job to give it to Adam. She invited them to practice kindness instead of judgement.

After she gave her brief talk to the students, the day had been as usual in the classroom. No big deal. He wore his hat in class and got on about the work of a Grade 1 student.

And as for how it went with all the other students at recess, it seemed it was a non-issue. He had enjoyed the playground with confidence, knowing that if someone should begin to tease, he could handle it because he had the permission note.

He hadn't given out a single one of those permission slips, but, even so, I believe they had powerfully done their job. I can't help but wonder if the confident tone of his stride had influenced how the other kids on the playground responded to his adorable comb over.

***

Permission slips are hugely valuable for parents to communicate with the school about what is best for their young children. I believe that it is hugely unfortunate that most of us use permission slips exclusively for such use. What if we all wrote permission slips? And not only for others, but for ourselves?

The reason they are good for children is the same reason they are good for adults—men and women, mothers and doctors, caregivers, professionals, and retired folk: Permission slips create space for a person to be human.

When a person gives themselves to be human, they relax. And when a person relaxes, their performance improves.

I work to do this in all sorts of situations—when I spoke at our local TEDX event in 2018, I gave myself permission to be terrified and intimidated even as I was excited.

When I joined a board recently, I gave myself permission to do more listening than contributing for the first meeting while I was getting acclimatized.

I also gave myself permission, in that meeting, to contribute periodically before I knew the complete back story and total context of every issue–as a bit of a perfectionist, that was a big one. In doing so, I was inviting myself to be brave without needing to be perfect.

***

I'm working to give myself permission these days considering of COVID-19. Permission to:

- Not get my "to do" list done that day

- Be disappointed that I can't go hug my adult kids

- Be upset that I can't go to a movie

- Be tired of all the ways COVID-19 is impacting my life

- Just simply find pandemic living hard

Sometimes, I give myself permission to feel tired or distracted, even while I'm about to work hard to do something important. It feels right not to have to pretend to be something I'm not. It doesn't mean I allow the fatigue to hi-jack me. I just allow it to be present, while I go about my business. I may give myself permission to feel hurt when my child has been nasty towards me—while also working to be the grownup. That permission often is a relief—the tired or hurt parts of me can stop demanding attention, and just be.

Other times, people might give themselves permission to:

- think about something without feeling pressure to respond right away

- not have to insist on being right all the time

- be candid about some concerns they have around a pandemic choice even though the thoughts aren't as clear as they would like

- take a deep breath and deeply listen to the other's concerns with no need to feel defensive or criticized

Almost always, I work to give myself permission to feel fear even when I'm being brave; to make mistakes even as I'm pursuing excellence; and permission to just be myself, even though I've never been, what I would consider, the *cool kid*.

There's something about writing one's own permission slips out. Just thinking it is good, but even better is watching your hand jot it down in ink on the paper.

Seeing it written somehow makes it real.

Permission slips are a strategy to be present with oneself. A person can write themselves a permission slip only once they know what they need. That often requires a deep breath and a mental check in with oneself. It's can be difficult, especially at first, but it's actually quite life-giving!

Creative prompts:

Ask yourself: Where do I need to be kind to myself and what would that look like?

Then, ask yourself: What do I need to give myself permission for right now? For what can I give myself permission to allow me to more fully show up and be my best self in this moment?

Give it a shot: Write out a permission slip. Write it on a post it note and put it on your bathroom mirror. Write it on the back of a business card and slip it into your wallet. Write it on the back of an old receipt you have in your pocket and put it back into your pocket. Pull out your notes app on your phone to tap it into your phone.

Go about your day, and mindfully be aware of that permission slip. Feel how it impacts you. How might you capture what happens when you write yourself a permission slip?

Nobody knows how to do a pandemic

D o you remember learning how to ride a bicycle? Remember how wobbly you were? Remember how you kept putting your feet down because you were losing your balance? You likely fell off your bike completely and skinned your knee once or twice. You had to run home to get a bandage for a bloody knee (or at least I did).

Once I learned to bike in a straight line, I had fun riding up and down the sidewalk in front of my house. However, the learning continued as I had to figure out how to turn corners on my two-wheeler, how to brake, how to slow down, how fast to ride given the conditions. It took a while to learn how to ride a bike.

I don't remember being angry with myself while I was learning. It was something new. I wasn't supposed to be good at something I was just learning. My parents let me know that falling was part of the process. They insisted I get back on my bike to try again—that falling was part of the learning. It didn't mean I couldn't do it, it just meant I wasn't good at it—yet.

I think living in pandemics is a lot like learning to ride a bike.

***

At the time of this writing, we are about 9 weeks into pandemic living. I'm getting the hang of things—or at least I think I am. However, the government guidelines here changed about 4 days ago allowing a different level of activity of business, with new recommendations about what is good for us. So, actually, I'm getting used to different levels of precautions—and I know they are likely to change as the numbers of those in hospital change.

I'm just getting to know who I am when I am living amid a pandemic. This is a unique stressor, and so I am responding in somewhat unique ways. Feelings such as grief, stress, anger cross all situations. For example, I'm familiar with how I respond to someone else's stress, and I am also somewhat familiar with how I cope during stress, in regular times.

However, I often cope with family stress by playing *hooky* for a night and I go to a movie all by myself on my way home from work on cheap Tuesday movie night. I only do this a couple of times a year but knowing I *could* do it increases my capacity for misbehaving kids the rest of the year too. Now, I know I can't. I also can't suggest that upset my son get some space and go chill with friends.

So many stressors—huge stressors—are impacting us individuals at the same time. Job loss, increasing debt, potentially life-threatening illness, deaths of family and friends close to us, some food or toilet paper shortages, closed stores—all at once. And so many stress relievers—gyms, movies, sporting events, concerts, restaurants, nail salons, the local bar, game nights with friends—are things we don't have access to (or limited access, depending on your area and stage of the virus) these days.

So many of the things we do to be good to ourselves aren't available.

And what is perhaps unique is that we have not collectively all faced similar challenges at this level since, perhaps, World War II. Being all in this together has its advantages and disadvantages. Again—unique.

One thing we have been doing around our house is to be students of ourselves. Given this unique situation of this pandemic, we are being re-introduced to ourselves. As we encounter a new stage, a fresh problem, a unique issue, a novel argument or discussion, we are endeavoring to learn something about ourselves.

I can't expect others to know how to relate to me during this pandemic if I haven't been present with myself to learn about how I "tick" in this new situation.

To that end, I have been working towards using **three phrases** with myself and others:

1. "What do you need right now?"

This one can take some thought. We don't always know what we need—because we aren't always aware of what's happening inside of ourselves.

My husband, Jim, often will ask me a more direct version of this question: "What can I do for you right now?"

He often specifically asks me this when he notices I'm stressed or overwhelmed or sad. And he leaves it open to me to teach him about what is helpful to me.

It's an amazing task—to imagine what I need that would be helpful, knowing he wants to know.

Sometimes, I have to ask him to wait a minute so I can figure it out.

It's a wonderful gift to be asked this question, although challenging. It's vulnerable to let someone (even oneself) know what you need.

I'm introvert and so often my answer these days is: "I need some time to myself." The amazing thing is that when he hears this, he smiles, nods (usually because he isn't all that surprised), kisses me on the forehead and walks out of the room. No resentment— just a demonstration of his understanding.

2. "What can I teach myself about me right now?" *or,* "Teach me about you right now"

I remember asking my son, in high school, a version of this a few weeks ago, as I extended my hands to him in a role play: "Ok, sweetie. This is me handing you a silver platter. I'm inviting you to place on it whatever insights would help me help you do schoolwork. Tell me what I need to know so you get the support you need."

Frankly, in that moment, it didn't work.

He didn't know.

But I think it was important to let him know that I was open to learning. I don't know what I'm doing as a homeschooling parent, and I want to be a student of him. Different kids will need unique sorts of supports from their parents.

It invited my son into a process of exploring what might work for him—because he is new to homeschooling. He has to experiment and try different strategies and find out what works for him.

3. "Thanks for telling me that. I like to know what works for you."

Again, my husband, Jim, taught me this one. This line usually comes right after I have told him something that doesn't work for me or when something I don't like happened. It's right after I've given him feedback that lets him know I didn't like something he did.

He, amazingly, often says this line *right after I've said something critical to him.*

Early in the pandemic, I had a pre-dawn live television interview via Skype. I still get a little nervous before television interviews because I don't do them often. This was my first Skype interview and so I was anxious because I wasn't sure how the technology would work—or even if it would work. International borders were closing and four of our children (two married couples) were going to be across the ocean, away from us for however long the pandemic lasted. They were going to stay there. These were not pleasant thoughts for me.

When it was time for bed, my husband prayed with me. He prayed at length about all the things I was worried about. He named my worries one by one—in detail. I got angrier and angrier as he was praying. I then got angry at myself because I was angry while someone was so kindly and earnestly praying with me and for me.

It took me until the next day to uncover the source of my anger. I didn't find it helpful for him to bring to mind all the fears I had and explore and expose them in his prayer. It felt like he was adding gasoline to the fire of my fears rather than extinguishing them by all the words he was giving to them just before we were to fall asleep.

He didn't get it—because he was just doing what he knew would be good—for him. But he listened, and he learned. And then he gave me this line: "Thanks for telling me. I want to learn more about how to be good for you."

So often, people would be tempted to get defensive or protest, or say how I was misunderstanding their intent or explain away the behavior.

And he just cheerfully says, "Thanks for telling me. That's good to know." It's like he is confident in himself and in my love.

So often, many of us would see this teaching: "This is who I am and what works for me," as an attack on our character or very worth as a human being when we hear it. For Jim, **it is information,** and he is grateful to me.

It startles me—and relaxes me—all at the same time.

Having the other adult in the house be open to learning about me increases my confidence in my ability to teach him about me, and frankly, makes me feel safer in my home. Because really, how is anybody supposed to know who we are and what our preferences are unless we teach them?

It is hard to tell people we care about what we need. It's so easy to stay silent and let others be unaware of how we are being hurt in a relationship.

How can I not want to steal that to use with others?

Creative prompts:

What have you learned about yourself and how you function during COVID-19?

When have you tried to you teach others about how you operate during this time and what happened? Maybe you'd like to be mindful of something you've learned about yourself and experiment with letting another know what works for you.

What are you learning about other people in your life and how they live, love and struggle during COVID-19? Can you give yourself permission to be a student of someone you know very well and learn something new about them?

Standard transmissions: RPM's

I've driven a standard transmission vehicle for many years. The motor idles at 800-1000 RPM's (rotations per minute). When the driver steps on the gas, the RPM's increase. The driver changes gears when the engine revs to about 3500 RPM's. The change to a higher gear decreases the RPM's.

Damage to a motor occurs when the motor is "red lined" at about 6500 RPMs. Drivers don't want to damage their motors, so they watch the RPM levels to ensure they don't get too high. A driver can hear the engine "scream" when the RPM's approach the danger zone.

COVID-19 has changed the "idling speed" of our internal engines. The background stress of the risk of illness, the losses directly and indirectly associated with this time increases our idling RPM's from 800 to idle higher—maybe 2000 or 3000 RPM's.

These are some factors that are increasing RPM's in the age of COVID-19:

- Parenting stressed children

- Homeschooling

- Working from home

- Not working at all

- Working on the front lines

- Shopping/errands

- Concern for the health of loved ones who are immunocompromised or have pre-existing health conditions, are elderly

- Loneliness

- Isolation

- Financial stress

- Landlord hassling you

- Technology hassles

- Technology overload

- Political division

- Family members with views of handling the pandemic that are different from yours

- Lack of social life

- Too many hours at home

- Inordinate amount of time at home/with family

- Stress over inability to physically distance because of elevators/compact living conditions

- Family member or friend ill with coronavirus

- Inability to "be there" for a loved one at a special occasion

Chances are that you can double the length of this list with stresses you face beyond this list.

What that means is, given all the stressors that raise your RPM's, it doesn't take nearly as much to "redline". The stress level created by the coronavirus reduces our resilience because there is much less room before it gets to the red line.

When our baseline level of stress is much higher, irritations and hassles that we can normally roll with will create reactions that seem out of proportion.

I am hearing from clients and friends and family that they notice themselves *losing it* on their kids and spouses. They are misplacing things or forgetting things—all signs of stress.

And ironically, they then *lose it* on themselves for *losing it*. Let's just say that doesn't help.

***

EXPECT those around you to be irritable and easily upset. Snapping back at them is understandable—because you are also irritable—but ultimately will only further increase RPM's.

EXPECT yourself to be short-tempered and easily frustrated. It's not only because you're at home with your family more and they are annoying. It's also because you are more easily annoy-able!

EXPECT yourself to want to numb yourself with screens and video games because it all seems too much to handle. EXPECT yourself to want to eat chocolate, or stuff carbs into your mouth, or drink one too many glasses of wine. This is your body's desperate attempt to lower RPM's when the external stress can't change.

EXPECT that if you don't allow yourself to name the stress and deal with it to impact your body. The body holds any stress that isn't acknowledged. The elevated RPMS's may show up in the form of neck and back-aches, headaches, upset stomach, toe tapping, knee jiggling, or nail biting.

***

Knowing that your body's RPM's are running high will help you edit your responses with others. Refrain from talking or texting when you notice yourself tipping into the "RED zone". Pull back—retreat—to lower your RPM's when you find yourself about to rip into your child, your spouse, your roommate.

When other's RPM's redlines and they explode on you, you don't have to passively accept their vitriol. If you are able to respond calmly and quietly, that will help lower their RPM's. You can let people know that if their RPM's are rising, you'll step away so you aren't subject to what might emerge when they redline.

What might have been something we could just absorb as inconsequential in our pre-COVID lives might now inflame rage.

We can handle stress better when we name it and understand its effect on us. When we recognize the impact of COVID-19 stress on our lives, we can make decisions about what we do with it—rather than have it rule our lives and ruin the lives of others around us.

What does it look like in your life to kind to your motor, monitor the RPM's and find ways that are good for it to be at a safe level?

As we name the obvious, we can figure out how we will manage this.

Creative Prompts

Go ahead—list all your stressors. The big ones, the medium ones, the little ones— even the miniscule ones. They are all valued—because they are what you experience. Leave room to add more tomorrow and the day after because I promise you, new stressors are coming!

What are the signs in your body that tell you that your RPM's are rising? Where do you feel it? What changes in your body shortly before you start "redlining"? Draw a picture of a person and use colored pencils/markers or paint to draw where and how you store your stress in the various parts of your body.

Stress is exhausting

I think it's reasonable to lower our expectations, people.

At the beginning of all this stay-at-home pandemic business, I set some goals. I planned to get a new website, write a book, take some courses and you know, all the things—home schooling, exercise, clearing out cupboards and organizing my files, board games with the family. I would have all this time, and it would be glorious.

I determined that I would be super productive; I would feel great about myself; and by the end of the pandemic, not only would my house be in order, but so would my kids, my career and my life.

I figured I would exploit this pandemic and use it for my own lofty purposes.

That was then.

This is now: My new goal is to floss my teeth every day.

I've recognized that I expected myself to be as, or even more productive than before COVID-19 and all its effects. That's not realistic.

Here's the thing: Stress on its own takes a lot of bandwidth. The stress of not seeing people, watching the people I care about struggle and not have a clue how to be helpful, figuring out how to make do without an ingredient or two for supper because I am not just running out to the store, ZOOM calls that zap energy, and knowing that 1000's of people in the world are dying from this without a loved one with them—all of that saps my energy.

It's not just me. Nor you. This is part of the trauma response, part of the stress we marinate in, all the time.

I remembered US Navy Admiral William McRaven's admonition in his graduation address: If you want to change the world, start by making your bed every day[3]. A humble task designed to give you a sense of accomplishment. Get one of the basic things done and do it well.

I translated that into: Floss my teeth every day. Something that my dental hygienist has been encouraging me to do for years, and something I haven't done regularly. My husband, Jim, started doing it, and I am just riding in his wake on it. And I've done it now for a few weeks, most nights.

We are both flossing. One new excellent thing that is coming out of COVID-19 for us—Score! This is a success that I celebrate (almost) daily.

Of course, I'm doing other things too. But I'm working to be gentle with myself and extend grace. I'm hoping to celebrate the bits of progress I make, rather than scold myself for all the time I squandered.

Ultimately, we will all be better off if we can honour what we are doing, rather than reprimand ourselves for all that we aren't.

I believe it is only when we accept ourselves for who we are and what we are able to do that we place ourselves in a position to do better—but only a little better.

Be realistic. *Really* realistic—COVID-19 realistic, not regular realistic.

Be good to yourselves, please?

Creative Prompts:

Whatever your expectations were at the beginning of this whole pandemic, you've likely lowered them. What were they then? What are they now? And explore—do they need to be readjusted again?

How and where have you noticed your "bandwidth" decreasing?

- Focus

- Attention span

---

[3] "If You Want to Change the World, Start Off by Making Your Bed - William McRaven, US Navy Admiral." *Youtube*, Goalcast, 17 Aug. 2017, https://www.youtube.com/watch?v=3sK3wJAxGfs.

- Fatigue levels

- Productivity

- Concentration

- Memory

- ??

What are the small concrete tasks that feel do-able for you these days? Have you been doing them? Have you been celebrating the victories? Congratulate yourself for all that you have done (regardless of what you haven't done.)

Stressin' about the stress

S kipper was my husband, Jim's, dog before I knew him. She was one of those hunting-type dogs—the kind that can and needs to run for *many* miles. An odd sort of dog to choose to have in the city, but they loved her.

Life at home was easier with Skipper after a good run. It wasn't easy to get her tired. If a family member looped her leash over the handlebars of a bicycle and went for a long cycle, Skipper could be in her glory. She would run long and hard for miles, and then the family could relax, because Skipper could have a long, happy snooze on her return.

There was an occasional wrinkle to Skipper's run—she **hated** lawnmowers.

It wasn't pretty.

Her hatred for lawnmowers was only matched only by her hatred of toasters. (Burnt toast once led to a piercing smoke alarm which led to a lifelong fear of all things being toasted—but that's another story. I digress).

The cyclist and Skipper would ride and run for miles and then they would suddenly come across a person mowing their lawn. With a lawnmower. And things would go sideways fast.

Skipper would **panic**!!

And when Skipper panicked, she did not run faster.

She stopped. Cold.

And her leash was attached to the handlebars. Of the moving bicycle.

Picture it. Yes, it isn't a pleasant, pretty picture.

The dog stopped. The bike, attached to the dog, stopped.

The rider, not attached to the bike, kept going.

And then the bike crashed, the rider flew over the handlebars and landed hard. The bike might land on or near Skipper with a crash. The rider would yell loudly in pain or surprise or both. The rider would direct the energy of the surprise, the fall and the resultant pain towards the dog. (Use your imagination here.)

And Skipper would look at the bike on the ground, at the rider with the new bruises and scraped knee, and the loud chaos that had just occurred. Then Skipper would look knowingly at the rider, as if to say: "See! Now do you understand why lawnmowers are scary? I told you lawnmowers are terrifying, and you wouldn't believe me!!"

***

I think we can all pull a Skipper on our own stress these days. I notice the evidence of my own stress—I see that I need an extra hour of sleep at night, or that I'm more irritable. It is hard and unfamiliar—and perhaps even frightening—to watch myself struggle with stress like this. I can tell myself all sorts of things:

- I don't have COVID-19, neither to my children, my parents or my friends—therefore, I am not allowed to be having a time of struggle. Shame on me.

- A stronger person could handle this better

- Feeling symptoms of stress is a sign of weakness

- Being tired is actually being lazy

These thoughts that I have about my stress create pain. Now, in addition to stressed, I am also disappointed, angry, feeling and ashamed.

Interesting, isn't it? I've been doing therapy for enough years to know that this is the universal story. In some form, you do this too.

Brené Brown says, "the "I'm not enough" explanation is often the first thing I grab, 'It's like my comfy jeans—may not be flattering, but familiar.' "[4]

---

[4] Brown Brené. *Rising Strong: How the Ability to Reset Transforms the Way We Live, Love, Parent, and Lead.* Random House, 2017.

It's telling ourselves the "not enough" story about our painful feelings that is often what really creates the pain. This isn't just a pandemic problem, it's a pervasive way of life.

I'm working to be aware of my stress and be compassionate towards myself. Kristin Neff is the North American guru on self-compassion—she literally wrote the book on it—Self-Compassion[5].

There are three components to self-compassion[6]:

Self-Kindness: Talking to myself like someone I love. Sometimes, when I notice myself saying nasty things to myself, I ask myself: "What would Mary say?" Mary is my Thursday morning latte friend. When she hears me struggle, she gently smiles and says, "Gee, this is hard. I see you trying really hard and still feeling like you fall short." After a while, she might also say, "Let's see what we can brainstorm to help you get through this"—but not right away. For a long time, she invites me to sit with her, as I feel her compassion and understanding. When I know how Mary would relate to me, then I can borrow her words.

Mindfulness: Taking a step back to watch myself in struggle. Mindfulness asks questions to give the situation perspective. If I ask myself: "Why am I reacting so strongly?" I may get some insightful response within myself that invites me to take helpful action rather than merely scold myself for my actions. Mindfulness reminds me that I have made it through tough situations before even when it felt like I wouldn't. Mindfulness is curious about what feeling is underneath the first feeling. For example, I might be tired which is creating my irritation, or fear underneath my stress.

Universality: We are all in this together. My suffering, my mistake, my stress, my pain—is something that others also experience. Others' suffering doesn't mean they are evil or inadequate or being judged. Their suffering means their circumstances are difficult.

In the pandemic, self-compassion sounds something like this:

Yes, this is hard. It's not hard because you're doing anything wrong. It's hard for you because it is hard. This pandemic is hard for everyone, just in different ways. Stress is part of the body's natural

---

[5] Neff, Kristin. *Self Compassion*. Hodder & Stoughton, 2013.

[6] Neff, Kristin. "Definition and Three Elements of Self Compassion: Kristin Neff." *Self*, Center for Mindful Self Compassion, self-compassion.org/the-three-elements-of-self-compassion-2/.

response because you are taking something seriously that deserves our concern. My shoulders are tight— maybe I can stretch them or put a hot water bottle on them. I don't think I've let myself breathe deeply for a while. Maybe I should get an app on my phone that will remind me to inhale slowly and deeply. I think I need to remind myself that I have gone through challenging times before, and I know how to do hard things. Maybe I will give myself the gift of not watching the news tonight so I can get a good sleep.

***

Marcus Antonius said:

"Consider how much more you often suffer from your anger and grief, than from those very things for which are angry and grieved"

Creative Prompts:

Notice what you are feeling. Then notice how you feel about your feelings. How are you unkind or judgmental about what is happening inside of you? In what ways you cause yourself suffering because of how you view yourself and your pain?

Write yourself a letter or draw yourself a picture. Send a message from the caring, most curious, clear and compassionate part of you to yourself about to address your suffering.

Anger, Blame and Judgement

This is not only a time of a disease—a virus threatening the health of all who come in contact with it. This is also a time of political divisiveness—our global community has caught the virus of discontent, judgement and criticism where folks are often more interested in partisanship than health; more invested in being right than making it right; and defending self-interest than the common good.

The stress of watching the news is just as much (or more) about political fighting and jockeying, accusations and counteraccusations than about the spread of the virus.

What happens when others cross it differently than we do? How do we deal with the feelings within ourselves when others craft policy or respond to policy so differently than we do?

The stakes are high. The virus is deadly. It has overwhelmed hospitals where the virus has silently spread. Inequities and injustices become apparent as the virus affects some communities more than others or as programs help some to the exclusion of others. The economy is tanking with record numbers of unemployed, and governments opening the tap wide open to spend money to help. Our children and grandchildren will pay for the cost of subsidizing the 2020 shut down for decades to come. Incredible uncertainty exists about the future of our economy—which will impact jobs; the ability to pay rent, buy groceries, get a mortgage; have investments and plan for retirement; and any other endless concerns.

Yes, the stakes are high—and so are emotions as we all seek to do the best for ourselves, our country, our world.

***

Think about it: What would you say if you were in your first trimester of pregnancy, you just arrived at Auschwitz Concentration Camp, and were standing naked with your head freshly shaved along with 100's of other newly arrived prisoners in rows in a courtyard—and Dr. Josef Mengele, (the "angel of death") looked at you and asked you this question: "Are you pregnant?"

During my socially isolated COVID-19 walks outside to get some air and space, I listened to *Born Survivors*[7], story of three women who arrived in Auschwitz early in their pregnancies who were asked this question. It was impossible—did admitting pregnancy save their lives or condemn them?

When faced with this decision, they thought fast and made a lightening quick decision. They each lied and denied the child growing in their womb. They could not know what the result would be.

With this decision, they lived.

They didn't—they *couldn't*—have all the information needed to make a knowledgeable decision. In fact, throughout their pregnancies, as they fought for their own lives and that those of their children, they had to constantly make the best decisions they could to survive—not knowing if it would lead to death or life.

My mind has often gone back to the grit of Priska, Anka and Rachel—these women who were making life decisions without having all the facts.

They made the best decision they could in an attempt to save their own lives, and the lives of their unborn—given the circumstances.

***

Here's the thing: we are in new territory. There can be no directive that says with certainty: This is the best plan. There are so many unknowns. The best experts we have are developing projections and forecasts which change regularly. There are inconvenient truths which sometimes are easier to ignore than highlight. Sometimes, the tension between opening the economy and the threat of the spread of the virus puts us between

---

[7] Holden, Wendy. *Born Survivors: Three Young Mothers and Their Extraordinary Story of Courage, Defiance, and Hope.* Harper Perennial, an Imprint of HarperCollins Publishers, 2016.

the ultimate rock and the hardest of hard places.

There is no way to extricate the world from this pandemic without a high cost.

A decade from now, when this pandemic is in our rear-view mirror, we will all have 20/20 hindsight. Now, the scientists and the medical team give us their best guidance given that no one has complete knowledge. And we do our best as individuals to apply the guidance to our own situation.

There is an incredible and seductive pull to turn on each other. To make others who come out differently than us the enemy. We can forget the virus is the common enemy. We can't see it or hear it—we can't punch it in the face after it kills someone we love. Of course, the pull it to find a face to punch—and then sock it to'em!

The pull is to relate to others out of our fear: the fear of the virus or the fear of economic devastation.

When we see others acts in ways we view as dangerous or unreasonable or overreacting, it is so tempting to become enraged. The automatic response is judgement: "I don't like what you are doing over there, as I yell to you from over here, where we do things right"

The virus of political division seems, someday, more likely to be the most devastating disease of this era.

Creative Prompts

Who have you been most angry with and why? Be bold to put it down on paper candidly. Let it out.

What cost does it have on you, personally, when you notice your own anger, judgement and blame at others?

What do you wish they would know about you and what is important to you they seem to miss?

What do you imagine those whom you judge might say you are missing about them and what is important to them?

Other problems continue

I wrote this on our Conexus Counselling Facebook page in March:

To the person who broke into my car last night,

I really felt like I didn't need to see that you had gone through my glove box and rifled through the various compartments of my vehicle this morning. I trust that you will make good use of the lone dollar coin that you found when you violated my car. Really, you had to give me a break-in when I'm busy coping with a pandemic? You didn't think I had enough going on? You thought it was a good idea to saddle me yet more?

These times are stressful enough with the COVID-19 virus on the top of everyone's mind. This is a week of transition for children to be home from school, toddlers from daycare, and employers from their place of business. I'm busy and already burdened, you see, with this stuff. I didn't need you to add further feeling of uncertainty and violation in my life.

But I have to admit, seeing my things—the pens and pins all over my car seat instead of their rightful place—reminded me of something important.

I think we are in danger of forgetting that many people are going through "normal" life stressors that they would face, even if there was no COVID-19. Folks are in palliative care; people who buried their spouse or a parent just last week; adolescents making desperately poor choices that create terror in the heart of their loving parents; and folks were at each other's throats before all of this started.

You know, the regular hugely painful parts of life. All that stuff is still happening. Regular everyday nasty stuff like car accidents, the water heater breaking down, seasonal allergies, and the toddlers with "terrible two's" continue even as the world has turned its attention to the struggle we all face together with COVID-19.

So, person-who-broke-into-my-car, your actions prompted me to be aware of those who have all the non-COVID-19 struggles of life **besides** the ones added in by the implementation of this week's chaos of social distancing measures.

I suppose, weirdly, I should thank you for that. It's been "all COVID, all the time" for many of us, making us near sighted to the suffering that some were in—and continue to be.

I suspect that there is some suffering in your life too, that had it seem like the best thing to break into my car. You know that you're better than that, and yet, that's the best you could do last evening. I pray for you, too, that you would get the support and care you need, too.

Be well,

Carolyn

Creative Prompts

What were your life's challenges before COVID-19 and how have they changed or stayed the same?

How has the predominance of COVID-19 in everyone's hearts and minds (including yours) impacted the suffering you bear over other life challenges?

Who else has a non-COVID-19 burden that you now remember may have got lost in the shuffle? What could you do to compassionately—to let that person know that someone sees their suffering?

What was true before continues to be true or even truer

In my career as a marriage therapist, I have told a spouse as a marriage was ending, "What made your marriage so difficult that it became no longer workable will now make the divorce difficult." They nod and smile, but I'm not sure they understand.

Months later, they return to tell me, "I get it now. The very factors which were hard on our marriage are now hard in the divorce. I may not have to live with the dynamics all day every day in my household, but those same issues are still the issues that complicate the divorce proceedings."

I think the same dynamic is at play during this time of COVID-19 pandemic:

- Toddlers who wouldn't sleep through the night with nightmares and had tantrums during the day are still up at night and having angry outbursts—and perhaps even more often.

- Colleagues who used to irritate you from the next cubicle with their late deadlines, their inaccuracies and their lack of attention to detail now unfailingly forget to mute themselves on ZOOM, don't send the information to you to allow you to do your part and when they do, still have errors. Only now, it's even more of a pain because you can't address it by standing up to peek over the cubicle wall

- Spouses that lost their temper and punished you with silence when you voiced your thoughts are still as angry—or angrier.

- The career driven person who was achingly lonely for true belonging now doesn't even have colleagues at work to chat with at the photocopier.

Conversely, the strengths of our previous lives can go with us into this current situation:

- A powerful bond between friends or spouses becomes even more vital during the crisis. The pandemic serves as a common challenge that unites them even more.

- The flexibility you have honed and practiced in your previous life assists you in pivoting to alternative business methods and new strategies for making it through this time.

- An interest in cooking evolves into an *all-out* passion for all things culinary. Neighbors rave about the sour dough bread they receive.

***

All of us lived our lives with quirky people, and quirky faults and strengths of our own. Painful relationships before continue to be painful during and after. The dryer finicky before is still finicky. The debt before that was worrisome now seems terrifying. The deliberate care you have made into creating a cozy home base now really has become a safe haven.

The implications of what was true before being as true or truer is this: We don't all experience the same pandemic in the same way. We all have challenges that made life challenging and difficult before and now continue to be challenges—molehills, hurdles, even mountainous problems.

That matters. There is no such thing as generic experiences during COVID-19. We all have a unique journey through COVID-19 land.

Creative Prompts:

What strengths in your life have become stronger in these last months?

What are the challenges that existed before that have made COVID-19 life uniquely challenging beyond what the common fears and risks that we are all facing?

What are difficulties in this time of COVID-19 that make life difficult specifically for you of which others may not be aware?

Grief

Daviid Kessler, a grief expert, recently had a profound interview with Dr. Brené Brown on her podcast, Unlocking Us. In it, he said this:

"We are all dealing with the collective loss of the world we knew. The world we knew is now gone forever."

I was out walking the neighborhood as I was listening, and this line stopped me dead in my tracks. I stopped to lean against a fence and pushed "30 seconds back" button three times to keep hearing it again.

Like the sun slowing rising to brighten the earth at dawn, we have increasingly come to realize that this isn't a two-week effort, or a one-month effort. This isn't something we could prevent: It is happening. We have lost thousands of lives to this virus. Thousands more will die. Tens of thousands of people are grieving the loss of a friend, a relative—loved ones. This is something that will shape our country for decades and will impact our world in permanent ways. There is no "going back" to a life we knew. The familiar, as we knew it, is gone.

You may have lost someone *near and dear* to you. You, yourself may have had COVID-19—with leftover symptoms you now must deal with. All of us have missed things we love to do, freedoms we used to have, and events that we can never get back.

Brené Brown speaks of three aspects of grief[8]:

Loss: Grief arises out of a hole that now exists in our lives. Something that belonged in our life—a person, an event, an activity, a relationship—is now not there. The hole matters. Ignoring it doesn't make it disappear. There can be a struggle to know what to do with that hole, how to handle its painful existence. It hurts to have it there—yes, it aches hard. It physically hurts to have the loss.

Longing: With grief comes the aching, soulful yearning. Beyond what we can consciously articulate, we long for what once was. Sometimes we scramble to substitute the longing with something else, other times we go back in time and sit with once was to reduce the ache of the present.

Lost: When that "something" or "someone" is gone, the usual and normal way of doing things is no longer possible. You roam an unwelcome and unfamiliar landscape physically, emotionally and spiritually. It's disconcerting to let go of something and be in a new and unversed in this unknown space.

There is so much grief that COVID-19 has created directly as a miscreant, and indirectly as a monster that has us all scrambling and turning our lives inside out to avoid its spread.

Many are resistant to calling it grief. A lot of folks find it too painful to name the losses as grief. Far too many express surprises as they receive the invitation to give themselves permission to name their losses as something to be grieved. Comparative suffering says: "You've lost a family member. I only lost my high school prom. I have no right to grieve." However, the greatest grief is always one's own grief and it matters. For some, this period has been the greatest time/event of loss in their lives—especially children. Not being able to play baseball or go to the swim championships may be the biggest loss yet.

"That which you feel you can heal" is a line many therapists know to be true. It more than rhymes; it reminds us how important it is to honor the loss. As you remember the loss, you remember the gift of having had it/him/her in your life.

Consider these losses:

- Friday night drinks with the buddies before you start the weekend

---

[8] Brown Brené. *Rising Strong: How the Ability to Reset Transforms the Way We Live, Love, Parent, and Lead.* Random House, 2017.

- Thursday night Grey's Anatomy nights with the girls

- A vacation over Spring Break

- The summer festivals that you look forward to every year which are now cancelled

- The wedding of a friend which you couldn't attend

- The funeral of a relative in another state that you couldn't fly to go to

- Not being able to visit your grandma in the nursing home or hospital

- Your high school or university graduation (or your son's or granddaughter's)

- Your child's tournaments, lessons, team practices—hanging out on the sidelines

- Alone time at home when everyone is out

- Together time with friends

- Getting your hair cut/colored

- Your job

- Your colleagues at your job

- Lunchtime walks with a work friend

- Banter during work meetings around the table

- Hugs with friends

- Attending professional sporting events in the stadium or arena

- Professional sports, period!

- Driving in the car to work (or taking the subway or public transport)

- Interesting stories from your partner about the day they had out of the house

- A movie at the theater with theater popcorn

- Working out at the gym

- Going to a public library, a bowling alley, the swimming pool, etc.

- Having your parents come to help with the kids

- Birthday parties

- Going to a crowded restaurant and feeling the buzz of all the people enjoying themselves

- Getting a pedicure

- Financial stability

- The big trip you've been planning for years

- Going to visit your people on a plane like you always do this time of year

- Sitting on the beach or in a park

- Being able to be out in public without concern of physical distancing

- The hope of being able to have enough for that down payment for your house or car next year

—and on and on and on, the losses continue

This is a long list. And incomplete—with each person able to double the length because of their own unique experience. This is loss—all of it.

And so, we grieve.

Creative Prompts:

If you have lost someone during the COVID-19 pandemic, know that this chapter is painful. A brief chapter in a short book is not enough. A few pages cannot begin to give you what you need to get through this. David Kessler has a daily online support group on Facebook for grievers to attend until "in person" support groups can resume. Maybe you want to hang out there? Give yourself lots of space to remember, to feel the enormous waves of pain that threaten to drown you. Know that others care. The ones reading these words right now—and myself, as I write them—extend our virtual hands of love to you in this moment.

Write out a list—major things, small things and all the things in between that you have lost during COVID-19. It will be an extensive list. You may be tempted to notice that you want to judge some it as trivial. Notice those feelings and be curious about them. I believe your entire list is important. You can both grieve what you've lost and still function in the day.

What has been the hardest loss for you during this time of COVID-19. Sometimes, the strangest things hit us hard. Perhaps write an obituary for that loss to honor it and the "next of kin"—yourself?

Second best has gotten old

It feels so inadequate to visit with my adult children on a computer screen or from the sidewalk. I'm frustrated with the weak links of video therapy when I can hear my voice echo a half second later in a maddening way. I'm weary from the business of Zoom meetings that may be productive business-wise, but lack any of the warm banter than in-person meetings have. I can still enjoy a good burger via takeout—but crispy fries just aren't as crispy by the time I get home.

I'm heartbroken people can only FaceTime with their relatives in nursing homes and can't hug them for fear of transmission. I ache for the people that find creative ways of visiting with their grandkids from a distance—but would just really rather sit them on their lap and read a story.

I ache when I see the pictures of two people "visiting" each other, through a window, each matching their outstretched hand against the others with a pane of glass in between.

Please understand—I **am** glad that we have technology for video and email. It gives me joy to leave supper at my kids' doorway. I enjoy posting a meme to someone I care about and couldn't otherwise contact. I can give my husband, Jim, a decent haircut, and part my hair ever more creatively to hide the grey. Second best works-sorta.

I have a hair appointment next week in our area, but it's not like old days. The receptionist warned me that I must first pass a screening prior to entering. I will wait in my car outside the salon until summoned inside. The door will be locked until they are ready for me. I'm invited to wear a mask. I won't get to play with Denim, the salon dog, while I wait my turn, and banter with Robert, the stylist, and the current customer still getting her hair styled. One customer at a time. I can hardly wait to get my grey gone, but it's sobering to think how different it will all be.

I can do second best because best is not an option right now. But make no mistake—I'd so much rather be hugging and eating and visiting and laughing and sitting with therapy clients and friends *in person*!!

If you ache with longing, feeling a little (or a lot) unsettled, you can remind yourself that there is still a lot to be grateful for.

But you can also still find this hard.

So, go ahead—Still miss that hug from your grandkids. Regret that you can't hug your aging mom. Find it hard that you can't eat with people you care about or enjoy that glass of beer at the pub together, or just pick up a carton of milk on the way home from work. Do the exercise class online. Feel the ache for all that has changed and all that you miss, and all that isn't quite right in your world.

It's OK to be finding these very creative "work around's" something to be grateful for, and yet very unsatisfactory. There is an understandable tension where both can coexist.

Second best is just that—second best. And we can grieve for what we want, even while we have a lesser form of it.

Creative prompts:

What are the clever "workaround's" you've come up with to continue something important to you, albeit not in the normal way? How have you and others been playful, even whimsical as you've *found a way*? Celebrate your creativity!

Give yourself a chance to be candid. Draw a chart with three columns. In the first column, write the activity that isn't the same now, even though possible in some fashion. In the second column, write your level of satisfaction of that activity on a scale of 1-10. In the third column, write your level of satisfaction that you have now. Now look at your chart and notice what is there. Can you extend compassion to the person who wrote those numbers and express empathy for how different the numbers are in the two columns? What else do you notice?

The time of pandemic as trauma

These are tough times.

Our brains are designed to look after quick emergencies—a fire on the stove, a child tumbling down the stairs, a car accident, being chased by a bear in the woods.

When that happens, our brains switch into *emergency mode* and we have high levels of energy to look after survival quickly and without thought. Our lightning fast limbic system overrides our cumbersome and methodical prefrontal cortex to take care of business.

COVID-19 is a different stressor—long term pandemic. It's been weeks and has no end date right now. Will it be months? Years? Our brains don't have opportunity to revert to a relaxed state, but rather remain constantly stressed. There is a level of being "keyed up" all the time.

Most of us are living in a subacute state of "fight/flight/freeze/appease" constantly:

Fight: People lose their temper more easily or are irritable. Family members cut a wide berth, never knowing when a person might snap. When the toast burns, a person slams it on the plate or closes the cupboard doors with more energy than necessary. The dog gets yelled at. Brakes get slammed. The newscaster receives snarling and derisive commentary back.

Flight: Sometimes this is about a physical energy to move. People get a little squirrelly. Need to get out and go for a walk. Long runs outdoors. Want to go for a drive. Sometimes, it's about creating distance between people: a person might leave the conversation when it isn't going well. The person doesn't show up for the Zoom meeting. Stay away from the invitations for connection.

Freeze: This is Netflix for hours. Not getting out of bed. Not showering or putting on clean clothes. Watching news in the evening and flipping from channel to channel knowing you should go to bed but then not moving.

Appease: This is *people pleasing* to fix the situation. This isn't authentic kindness, it is pasting a smile on your face and looking like you are cooperating and happy even when everything inside of you is terrified. It's avoiding the danger by not antagonizing the perpetrator.

Living in fight/flight/freeze/appease has some practical implications. As your brain is stressed and surveying for danger in a vigilant way as the priority, it is less capable of dealing with the mundane. This means you may have less ability to concentrate in meetings, the recipe or the homeschool app. You might be easily distracted or have less focus. You might make silly mistakes that are uncharacteristic.

I'm not getting as much done these days as is my usual style. I have difficulty sitting down to get my usual output for work.

When a person's body is feeling in a constant state of alert because of trauma, their bodies get distressed. It affects heart rate, blood pressure, insulin levels, the ability of the body to fight infection.

We recognize a person is in trauma when they are in a situation that is of intense (or perceived intense) danger for them or for someone they love or are present with—and they are helpless to make it safe.

***

To be clear: nobody can yet have *Post* Traumatic Stress Disorder for COVID-19 at the time of this writing. We are still **in** the period where safety does not yet exist. So often we find ourselves helpless to fix something we know to be important for ourselves or someone we love:

- A person sees a nurse-colleague break down in tears, and that person doesn't go hug him/her as would be automatic. Instead, that person overrides their natural impulse and stay physically distant, helpless to do what they know to be the profoundly human and right action.

- Life at home is contentious and stressful. Everyone in the household is snapping, and tempers are getting close to the boiling point. The natural response would be to leave and let things cool down. Everything in a person says: "Go for a walk and cool off. Don't let this escalate." But the elevator access high-rise apartment in a crowded city doesn't allow for the opportunity to get fresh air given the restrictions. So, the person stays in the pressure cooker, unable to get out of the way so it doesn't explode.

- Your daughter is single parenting 3 kids, while homeschooling the two oldest. She is also working from home (or trying to). She is overwhelmed, exhausted, and her nerves are understandably *fried*. You love your daughter and your grandchildren, and it's normal to go over several times a week for a few hours to help. Now, you must stay away and watch her struggle on her own. She is drowning in her life and besides reading to the kids via Facetime; you are helpless to help.

- Nurses want to invite family members to be present with a dying COVID-19 victim but can't allow family to come. They work to provide a video call and hold the dying person's hand—except they have multiple patients. Pressing needs force the nurse to leave someone who needs them to someone else who also has a critical need.

Times of trauma are hard and confusing. The fear is acute. Often people may not realize the effects of trauma until it is long past. Other times the experiences which appear so terrifying end up not having a long-term traumatic effect on a person.

As always, people in trauma need support. Folks deal best with trauma when they know they are heard and understood and someone cares that they are feeling so scared and helpless. Naming the trauma to someone who is loving and caring and deeply understanding is beneficial.

Creative prompts:

Of the fight/flight/freeze/appease approaches to traumatic situations, which one do you find yourself using most often these days? Most people use all of them at some point—can you think of an example for each?

Write the time(s) when you have felt that you have been utterly could not do something to help yourself or another that was very important to do, but forbidden given the circumstances. Name them. Describe what the situation required, and what you really wished/absolutely needed to do. Can you call someone you trust to listen carefully as describe those situations to them?

Grounding

These days, information is coming so fast, so often, and frequently, so inaccurate that it's easy to get freaked out about COVID-19.

Conspiracy theories lift our feet off the ground, and we float away from truth—when those theories are debunked, we may or may not hear about it. False theories tend to come in a much louder way than they leave. We can spend valuable energy worrying about faulty science or groundless rumors.

News about COVID-19 is on every station regularly. News networks are all COVID-19, all the time. If we want to obsess and spin in the vortex of dreadful news about COVID-19 in our world, we have the capability of endless news stories, podcasts, Facebook posts, Reddit threads, and YouTube videos.

We lift up and away from our best selves and feel adrift. We lose our sense of groundedness.

Friends, this is not helpful.

In times where there is uncertainty, we need to remember all that hasn't changed: Smile are welcome. Love abounds. You have eyes that see and ears that hear. Your family and friends still love and care about you. You matter to them; they matter to you. We all take care of each other.

Staying grounded is a way we look after ourselves and each other. Grounded people buy what is prudent, rather than panic purchase. Grounded people don't freak out when they watch others freak out.

I received a message from a therapist who said that one way she is coping is that she asked her daughter to change her passwords on social media. She limits how much she can expose herself to alarmist rhetoric. She is more available to her family in body and spirit.

Ground yourself. It is a kindness to yourself and others. A few tips:

- Limit the number of times per day you watch news. Being caught up on the latest does not require repeatedly assaulting your nervous system with repetitively exposing yourself to the constant barrage of information available.

- Limit social media. Unfollow sites and accounts that make your heart race or throat tighten.

- Avoid couch potato-ing your way through this—binge watching numbs and is the opposite of grounding

- Help someone. Focusing on what you can do reminds you—you are not helpless.

- Go for an extended walk outside. Or a short one. Or even stand outside your door and breathe in cold, refreshing air and feel the natural light. Nature is good for us.

- Breathe[9]. Slowly and deeply. From your belly. Multiple times throughout the day.

- Google "yoga class" and try it. There are many that are available. Give yourself the gift of centering yourself.

- Do normal things. Make a meal. Play a game. Watch your usual show (one episode-not 6). Clean out a closet.

- Find a pet to snuggle.

- Ask for help. Talk about the spins in your head out loud. Thoughts in our head can whirl tighter and increase anxiety—saying it out loud to someone unspools the thoughts and organizes them. It will help you plan in a calmer way.

- Dance. Yes—Dance! Move your body to your favorite music. Leap, jump, gyrate, jiggle, sway, tap and swing yourself around. Raise your pulse in rhythm to the music. Feel your body unload the excess energy in ways that celebrate your body's ability to move.

---

[9] Klassen, Carolyn. "Take a Deep Cleansing Breath... - - Winnipeg Manitoba." *Conexus Counselling*, 16 Mar. 2020, conexuscounselling.ca/2020/03/14/cleansing-breath-covid-19-virus/.

- Deliberately switch your mind from all that feels out of control to what you know is within your control. Find a tiny thing that you can have agency over by doing a kindness for a neighbor, or some small goodness for yourself

Let's take care of each other—and that starts by taking care of ourselves. Keep your feet firmly planted.

Creative Prompts

What do you do to give yourself a sense of being grounded? What are the practices you have adopted that are good for you? Reflect on what makes these strategies good for you.

Try a new grounding strategy from the list above. Pick one you're not as familiar with using and give it a shot. What happened?

Risk Averse and Risk Acceptant— Yours, Mine, Ours

I've had friends who have gone bungee jumping and loved it. Other people I know have jumped out of an airplane and found it exhilarating! Parasailing, scuba diving, mountain climbing—many people love some or all of these.

Me? Nope. None of them. They might be fun, but those are risks I just don't find worth it. I'm *risk averse* to these.

Those who do these extreme sports might not understand my reticence. They enjoy the thrill of these activities. They feel alive and vibrant as they engage in wild adventure.

However, I believe I do brave and risky things. I married a second time after my heart broke at the end of my first marriage. I have flown on an airplane halfway around the world to a country I had never been to explore it. I've hosted a radio show a twice when given an opportunity. Last week, I gave my first seminar via video, even though I was nervous about it to about 80 people.

Each of these felt risky. I was both scared and brave as I decided to *go for it*. I was *risk acceptant*.

Others might decide that any of these is too great a risk. The possibility of failure or adverse outcome was not something to which they wanted to expose themselves.

Some might consider me risk averse. They might whisper about me to say I am cowardly or a wuss. Others will see me as risk acceptant. A lot of it would depend on their own capacity and comfort for risk in their own lives.

***

Some individuals can hardly wait to have an ability to be more *out and* about in this time of pandemic. Others are more hesitant about changing their level of social isolation. Some businesses want to protect their employees with being more cautious with re-opening. In my city, some businesses establish guidelines more stringent that the government has outlined.

You may be willing to accept the risk of disregarding physical distance, either because you are risk acceptant, or because you perceive the risk higher to stay away from your employment. Work or get fired. Work or lose your apartment. Perhaps the cost of social isolation is so high, you will see government guidelines more as *suggestions* with which you use with some flexibility. Some business owners are figuring out a way to open within guidelines—or even outside the guidelines.

No one wants to be sick die from COVID-19, nor have any of their relatives meet that fate.

No one wants to have our global and national economy sink into a depression. No one wants to lose their business, their car, their house, their education.

We all fall somewhere on the spectrum of risk acceptance to risk averse.

In this time, there are multiple vectors that one is finding their sweet spot of acceptable risk:

- The likelihood of becoming ill and/or transmitting COVID-19

- Our need for social connection/contact with those who need us

- Our need to exchange goods and services to earn income

Each of us is assessing risk and reward in our behaviors on these factors. We come out at different places as we have differing levels of comfort with risk, and different priorities and commitments in our lives.

Here's the rub: there are very few situations in which my neighbor's comfort level of risk so clearly and immediately impacts my own risk and exposure. As others are comfortable being out, and willing to accept risk of infection spread, it seems they are choosing to increase the risk for others.

My actions have always influenced the lives of others. Yours too. But now, more clearly than ever, we are seeing that my choices around risk directly impact your risk. Your choices may directly impact the safety of my children who work on the front lines.

***

I wrote this on my Facebook page last week:

I spoke to a woman who lives with someone for whom the COVID-19 illness could well be life-threatening. The family member has a medical condition that places her at very high risk for the worst sort of COVID-19 expression.

This family is hunkered down at home and is settling in for the long haul. They will maintain strict isolation to save her life.

This is hard. And lonely. No contact with anyone they love or that loves them. No shopping. No errands. *Nothing.*

And, in the evenings, they watch the families on the sidewalk outside their home. Families passing by with rambunctious children on little bikes or scooters. Other families out for an evening stroll. A couple walks by, hand in hand. A runner jogs by. Intermittently, they see people coming from the left and from the right, simultaneously.

Families come towards each other from opposite directions. And, in a way that literally brings this woman to tears, she watches as one family goes up on the grassed yard, while the other family steps off the sidewalk onto the street. The sidewalk is empty between them.

She watches people choose to leave the sidewalk to each go out of their way to create physical distance. Perfectly healthy families, for whom the risk outside is low, move apart according to provincial guidelines.

When she witnesses the people creating distance, she knows she is not alone in the burden of keeping her family member safe. The community comes together as they stay apart.

She watches people helping her to save the life of someone she loves, lives with and can't imagine living without. When there are so few ways of feeling the support and love of others, they get to feel the love every evening as they look outside on the sidewalk outside their house.

She wanted you to know this. She wanted you to know that you become part of the health care team for folks with serious medical conditions when you get off the side.

You need to know that you give hope when you physical distance. The ones who live knowing this virus can ravage their loved ones need the hope you give.

She wanted me to thank you. So, I am. Thank you.

***

This time is a challenge as our level of objective risk (e.g. pre-existing conditions) and our level of personal comfort regarding risk averse/acceptance meets someone else's level or risk and risk acceptance in the park/store/workplace. Managing how to live respectfully as a community when others have different levels of risk is a huge endeavor.

Creative Prompts

Where do you generally fall on the spectrum of risk averse to risk acceptant? What influenced how risky a person you are in life? Does your pattern throughout your life match your tolerance for risk now during the virus?

How do you decide how much to let the risks others are facing—and their own perceived level of acceptable risk—impact the way you alter your behavior? How have you made choices to protect others even when you felt it wasn't important for yourself? When have you chosen to do something because it felt important and acceptable even though others would not want you to?

Think about the tensions that exist as people handle risk differently and the divisiveness this can create. How are you a part of the problem? How are you a part of the solution?

This math doesn't work for parents

he math doesn't work for parents—and I'm not talking about grade school new math or twelfth grade precalculus, which parents are now responsible for as home school teachers!

T I was listening to an interview with a human resources consultant as she was describing her manager coaching strategies as people were shifting to working from home. She said that managers were trying to figure out how to supervise employees. These staff were parents, who were also homeschooling kids at home while trying to work full time. Her suggestion to managers was to suggest to parents to be flexible by putting the kids to bed and then putting in two hours of work between 8 pm and 10 pm.

Yep. Work for hours after the kids go to bed. All I could shout at the radio was: "THIS IS UNREASONABLE!" During a pandemic. Somehow, this would solve a problem. I'm thinking: "This will create problems!!"

This pandemic is stressful on parents–they are more irritable, have less ability to focus and concentrate, need more *down time* and more sleep. Parents have less to give–and yet are required to give more than ever. Zoom meetings, being interrupted at home, alternate work strategies because the decentralized office.

This time of pandemic stresses kids out. Thus, they need more cuddles, more books read to them, more support to do any kind of schoolwork out of the classroom, more active games, more room for stress tantrums and short tempers. Their difficult behavior says: "This is hard and scary, and I need some help to feel safe!"

And we are all feeling the stress of the virus. This is not only parents' first pandemic, it's also the kids: Wash your hands. Stay 6 feet away. Pull the kids away. Explain to the kids. Remind the kids. Remind them again. Worry about the family member who is a front-line worker. And remind the kids to wash their hands again–no, longer–you haven't washed them long enough.

There was hardly enough of most parents of young children to go around before COVID-19. And now–the demands just increased, exponentially.

How is a person supposed to be a full-time employee while having no childcare, and now teaching your child full time–while the child and you are both in a newly stressful situation?

The math does not work.

If you are a parent of young children at home, you might be at snapping point. You may have been at the breaking point two weeks ago—and there was no relief then, none now, and we don't know when you will be able to get the support you need. This must be beyond overwhelming.

Know this: We see you. Speak up. Don't be a superhero. Don't let yourself get run into the ground.

If you find:

- Something is too much, let the boss know.

- The children are watching too much screens, know that it might be better than the alternative.

- You feel yourself getting so tired and so frustrated, you don't trust yourself to parent safely, call someone and say so. I and so many others will not judge you. It would be an act of courage to pronounce your limits.

A friend of mine, Rose, had a husband that travelled a lot when her children were young. Her kids were rambunctious and curious. They were a handful and she was overwhelmed as most of us moms with young children were. When her husband would leave on a trip, the kids knew this: they would have ice cream for supper. They had fruit to put on it—but ice cream wasn't dessert—it was the meal. The children looked forward to ice cream for supper when daddy went away. It made the hard day of his departure a little less hard for them—and thus, for their momma.

Rose gave herself permission to do something fun and easy to make going through a hard time do-able. These children are now in their mid-20's. They are healthy and athletic. They are strong and eat well. Her kids remember those ice cream suppers with fondness, and they are none the worse for wear.

Can you give yourself permission to do what it takes to get through another day with more on your plate than can you can possibly deal with? Maybe crawl under the kitchen table and read books to them for hours if that's all you can manage? Make a blanket fort and eat crackers and cheese and watch a movie under there? Can you imagine how taking a break from responsible living might be a memory the kids will cherish in the future?

I'm sorry this is so hard. This isn't fair to you. Take care.

Creative Prompts

If you don't have small children, take a few moments to imagine how the time of COVID-19 might be different if you were parenting a couple of anxious kids during this time. Take a minute to write a note of encouragement to a parent, or even make a casserole to drop off at their door for supper tomorrow.

If you have children: take a deep breath. Imagine myself and the other readers who are reading this chapter extending a warm hand and a friendly smile of support to you. We know how stinking hard this is for you and it matters to us. We are wanting to encourage you. We extend our compassion toward you. We invite you to do something that will be good for you and safe for the kids that is silly, fun and free.

We can learn a lot from children about how to go through a difficult time. I remember watching a 7-year-old girl play tag with a friend in the foyer of the church before her dad's funeral began. She was about to enter a long service of intense sadness and she was being a playful child with a bit of "normal". What sort of playful whimsy might be fun for you? The more ridiculous the better.

- Brainstorm.

- And try one.

- And reflect on it after.

Boundaries

B oundaries—what is OK and what is not OK—are tricky in the age of COVID-19. The rules for boundaries have drastically transformed.

We are all trying to catch up with new boundaries, shifting boundaries, and dealing with all the pain that results when your boundaries are violated and disrespected.

We see news stories of people resisting authorities mandating certain levels of restrictions for gathering together. "Don't tell me what to do", or "It's my right to decide" are statements by folks who feel like their personal freedoms—their boundaries—are being violated.

We watch Personal Protective Equipment (PPE) being used not only in hospitals, but in grocery stores and on the street. People creating a boundary of protection to prevent the spread of the coronavirus. We watch others express fear and distress when they need the boundaries of masks and face shields to prevent infection and they aren't able to acquire it.

What used to be perfectly acceptable can now be deadly:

- Handshakes

- Being in a crowded arena cheering a sporting event

- Attending a funeral

- Touching surfaces others have touched without it first being cleaned.

Government guidelines are asking us to stay apart to "flatten the curve" in ways that feel odd and challenge our long-accepted standards relating to others.

When I walk down the street, people see me coming and move off to the side. I know it's for my good. It's an act of respect. But why do I feel like I'm in 7 years old all over again, and I'm at recess and someone is shouting, "Hey everybody, Carolyn has cooties. Everyone—run away from Carolyn's cooties!" There is something primal in me that feels a pain when people pull away from me.

I sometimes wonder if we can really recognize the price we pay at a deep level beyond conscious awareness to have people pull away, stay away, back off, and armor up with masks against each other.

***

Personal and professional boundaries are shifting, and change is required, and not always with enough discussion to ensure that the new boundaries that become established work effectively.

The few relationships in your life that you have with people in your immediate space have now become the only face-to-face relationships that many of us have.

Roommates or spouses may work from home and doing everything else at home too. The natural rhythm of going out to the gym, or out with friends, or out to book club isn't happening. Suddenly, those that live in your house are your work colleagues, your friends, your confidantes, your sources of entertainment, the only ones with whom you can argue or converse with. That's too much weight for most relationships to hold. The strain builds—until there is a snapping.

Domestic violence has increased during this time of COVID-19. Home is a frightening place for many—and now it's a place that they can't leave.

***

Extroverts struggle with these new boundaries: No concerts, no crowded bars, no movies, no public gatherings of any kind. Depending on the stage of precautions, perhaps no guests in your home, or ability to go to restaurants. This is an extrovert's nightmare. Extroverts look to be with people to be energized—and opportunities to be with others is in short supply.

This is no picnic for introverts either. For people who like and need "alone time" it feels impossible. Those who live with a family have no time alone. There is no evening where everyone is out at activities, or a quiet house while everyone else is at school or work. People around every moment of every day. An introvert's nightmare.

***

Boundaries impact work from home.

You may have met your boss' dog, or your colleagues' kids as they scampered in during a video call. You have a sense of what one wall of their house looks like. That may be interesting—or too much information. You may know far too much about what their nose looks like as you look up their nostrils for an entire meeting.

There is no drive home from work to decompress before you see your family after work. No time to transition from work mode to home mode. In fact, there is no transition at all. How do you turn work off when it remains right there at home?

You may not feel comfortable working at the hospital or the drug store—but need to work. You work in an environment where you don't feel safe.

Boundary establishment and boundary enforcement is a challenge when public guidelines for boundaries shift regularly, and we struggle with what is ok and not ok in our lives at every level.

Creative Prompts

How does your body feel/react when others pull away or stay away from you? What is it like for you to avoid people in a way that we would have said is unnatural before this pandemic?

What have you done to name and let others know about your boundaries? What have you done to let others know about your boundaries in this new landscape?

What further work would you like to do in your life to further clarify in your life "what is ok and what is not ok"?

Skin hunger

You might never have heard the term, "skin hunger", but intuitively, you know what it is, right?

Many of you could REALLY use a hug. A long and friendly and warm hug of comfort.

And you won't get it.

Hugs, except amongst those within households, are scarce. Non-existent. And we don't know when they are coming back.

***

When Jim's late wife died, he went out for breakfast with a friend who had lost his wife in a tragic accident the year before. They went out after Jim's wife, Car, had passed away but before the funeral. The friend's advice: "Take all the hugs you can get in the next few days. Nobody hugs a widower after the funeral is over."

That bit of advice stuck in Jim's mind. You can hear the ache in the words of this fellow a year after his own wife's funeral, I think. The skin hunger that comes from losing a wife's warm embraces and feeling that while others might care, they don't give hugs.

***

To remain unhugged when you could really use a hug is a very hard thing.

There can be a real internal ache that arises out of needing the warmth of human touch. Simply, the need to be touched is very real.

We all need to be touched. Our brains become soothed with contact. Hugs relax us when we are stressed. Tender touch is calming and nurturing in ways that are essential.

One of the most common ways we extend comfort people experiencing stress is a hug, an arm around the shoulder, or placing our hand on their hand. We are not permitted to physically receive of extend comfort to someone outside of our home these as part of physical distancing.

I regret that this is the way our world needs us to be. To protect our physical health, we compromise emotional and social health.

I have to remind myself sometimes that I am not being cold and callous when I hold myself back from a hug. Before COVID-19 when I would greet a friend, I would often offer an embrace of greeting and of good-bye. Especially if I knew they were having a hard time, I would immediately give them a warm, friendly squeeze. Now I don't. It feels rude. It's an odd world to live in that not hugging someone is the kind thing to do.

My mom asks when stop for a visit from the porch, "Can I give you a hug?"

I can tell she wants one. And I turn her down. That feels wrong. Very wrong. Even though it's the right thing to do.

Our brains release oxytocin when we have skin to skin contact. Oxytocin is the "tend and befriend" hormone that calms and soothes. Oxytocin can actually shut off the stress response. Neuroscience understands that hugs make a difference to calm our brains.

This would seem to present an issue then for people who live alone. How are they supposed to get the touch that is so essential for turning off the stress response?

I was listening to a podcast that Jen Hatmaker hosted[10] with Dr. Hillary McBride[11],

a therapist. Dr. McBride says:

There was some research that was done a few years ago, that showed, for people when they were measured for rates of oxytocin that were released. There was actually no difference, or a very slight difference in how much oxytocin was released when they touched themselves vs when they were actually touched by someone else. So, it seems like your body is like, "Oh I'm connected to somebody, even if it's YOU!" Isn't that beautiful?

I would just encourage all the people who are alone to know it is just as good… that your brain

---

[10] "Dr. Hillary McBride's 7 Steps to Grasp Big Feelings During Hard Times." *Jen Hatmaker*, jenhatmaker.com/podcast/quarantine-bonus-series/dr-hillary-mcbrides-7-steps-to-grasp-big-feelings-during-hard-times/.

[11] "Therapist, Researcher, Speaker and Writer." *Hillary L McBride*, 25 Sept. 2019, hillarylmcbride.com/.

doesn't care if you are giving yourself a hug. We have come up with stories to disqualify why that matters.

But it matters.

Dr. McBride suggests that those who aren't able to receive touch from others find ways to provide nurturing touch to themselves. Touch such as:

- Cup your face lovingly with your hands, as a mother might to a small child

- Rest your head on the palms of your hands when you are weary

- Put one hand over your heart and feel the thump

- Wrap your arms around your belly in a self-hug

- Give yourself a foot rub

- Massage the back of your neck

As you provide gentle and caring touch on your body, be mindful. Be fully present as you feel your hands on your skin.

I love the idea that we can in some sense provide that touch for ourselves. While it's not the same as a hug from another, it's helpful and meaningful.

Your need for touch matters. Your body longs for gentle and caring touch.

Creative Prompts

Do you need a hug? From whom? Spend some time giving yourself permission to long for a hug from the people whom you love. What would that hug feel like? What would it do for you?

Do you have people in your life that really want a hug from you and yet you aren't able to provide it? What is it like to want to care for someone with a sign of physical affection and then hold yourself back from that touch? What does it cost them? What does it cost you?

Try touching yourself in a kind and gentle way, feeling the tenderness you are extending to yourself. Soak in the care you give yourself. Reflect on the experience.

Disconnection is painful and connection is healing

I believe we are wired for connection. Relationship is what give purpose and meaning our lives. When I provide therapy to clients, I do so with the picture of Michelangelo's Creation of Adam[12] hanging above their heads. It is there to remind myself that regardless of what we discuss that is of concern for the client, if we keep peeling back the layers, we will discover that there is a component of connection/disconnection.

I believe so strongly that we need relationships that when I received an invitation to apply to give a TEDx talk, my idea worth sharing was, of course, the idea that, "We are wired for connection". In the talk, Learning from the Sequoias: the Value of Interconnectedness.[13]
Part of what I said was:

> *When I went to California for graduate studies in marriage and family therapy, I couldn't have imagined that my most powerful lesson on relationships wouldn't be in the classroom, but in a forest.*
>
> *On weekends off from studying I would travel around the state to see its beauty. My favorite*

---

[12] "Michelangelo's Creation of Adam." *ItalianRenaissance.org*, www.italianrenaissance.org/michelangelo-creation-of-adam/.

[13] "Learning from the Sequoias: the Value of Interconnectedness Carolyn Klassen TEDxWpg" *Https://Www.youtube.com/Watch?v=S9BJjkijb2I&Feature=Youtu.be*, TEDx Winnipeg, 2 Oct. 2018, *https://www.youtube.com/watch?v=S9BJjkijb2I&feature=youtu.be*

and most memorable visit was to the King's Canyon National Park, where I saw some of the largest living organisms on the planet: Sequoias trees. These majestic trees can grow more than 80 meters high—that's roughly as high as a 24-story building—and be as wide as 10 meters in diameter. These monstrous trees are able to withstand the roughest weather, and some have done so for more than 2000 years.

Incredibly, the roots of sequoia trees go down into the ground only about ½ to 1.5 meters. It would seem impossible—and yet, is obviously, and remarkably, possible, for them to remain standing. But here's the thing—a giant sequoia never grows alone—always, always in a grove. A sequoia weaves its roots in and amongst the roots of other sequoias over time, covering as much as an acre—to create incredible stability…and then these trees actually connect their roots to each other—joining together—so they can help each other out.

A key to the sequoia trees' survival is their interconnectedness.

Sequoia trees need each other.

They are wired for connection.

People are no different. We are wired for connection—we need each other to survive and thrive. We were meant to grow in a forest of humanity; to have lives around us intertwining with ours. People enjoying each other in the everydayness of life, and also ready and steady when circumstances threaten to bend us, ensuring we don't topple over completely in the inevitable storms of life.

Research has found that women with breast cancer with a large network of friends were 4 times more likely to survive as women who were not as connected.

Swedish research found that those with extensive social networks have a lower rate of dementia.

John Cacioppo and his colleagues found that when people had active social lives they recovered faster after illness.

Julianne Holt-Lunstad's analysis of 148 studies found that people that have better social connections have a 50% reduced risk of early death. The risk of social isolation is comparable to smoking 15 cigarettes a day and carries more risk than obesity or air pollution.

Strong bonds help cardiovascular health, strengthen immune response, keep brains sharp, and slows cellular aging.

Relationships are an integral part of mental health.

Robert Waldinger, the current head of Harvard Study of Adult Development, says that the clearest and most conclusive message that we get from this 80-year study is that: "Good relationships keep us happier and healthier. Period."

Entwining our lives with good friends has really practical implications as well: We make better food choices when we eat with others, and we show up at the gym when a friend is meeting us there.

Friends remind you to do the things the doctor told you to do or check in on you during a rough patch.

My friend, Mary, is that type of friend for me. Tomorrow, we will get together for morning coffee, as we have on Thursday mornings almost every week for 14 years. Unless one of us has specifically cancelled, I show up.

She shows up.

We show up for each other—to talk, laugh, and sometimes cry. Usually we talk about the mundane, beautifully ordinary moments of life: parenting, work, aging parents.

If something significant happens to one of us, Thursday is coming, and it will get talked about, with all the rights and privileges that are granted with deep depth of friendship.

In forest language, we are old growth friends.

I am a better version of me because of Thursday mornings with Mary.

***

I feel like people understand how we are wired for connection more now than two years ago when I gave that TEDx talk—not from watching the video, but from our current reality. The coronavirus has us acutely aware of how wired together we really are.

Many of us stay home knowing if we get the virus we are likely to remain asymptomatic but could then pass it onto others for whom the disease could be serious, even fatal. We have had to lean on each other and help each other out in unprecedented ways. We recognize the people who have too often been overlooked as inconsequential, like bus drivers, grocery store clerks and long-distance truck drivers. These are now considered important and essential front-line workers. We truly do need each other, and we are more aware of this than ever before.

***

I'm grateful for this nation-wide awareness. Our culture was becoming increasingly isolating:

From the TEDx talk:

However, meaningful relationships are becoming an increasingly endangered way of life. Research says that the number of close confidantes that people have, has dropped in the last couple of decades. Social media has made us a people with more acquaintances and fewer friends. Many find themselves in a position where they have hundreds with whom they can share a photo, but very few, if any, with whom they can actually celebrate the joy, or mourn the sorrow, behind that photo. In this age of social media, roots go down and out, but don't intertwine in the way that authentic face to face encounters nurture and develop.

In the 2016 census of Canadian households, for the first time in history, single person households, at 28%, surpassed any other type of household.

The 2017 Vital Signs report by the Winnipeg Foundation reports that 37% of people in our city were sometimes, often or always lonely in the past week.

Meaningful relationships develop out of the gradual braiding together of lives. Trust develops, with gradually deepening exploration by vulnerably and authentically sharing life's joys, struggles, tensions, losses, and victories with each other. We are loved, not in spite of our quirks and foibles, but because of them.

It is, then, a huge irony and something of great distress that at the precise time that we are more aware of our interconnectedness than ever, that we are also required to:

- practice social/physical distancing,

- refrain from going outside too often, or at all,

- gathering in large groups to mourn or celebrate,

- stay home from being friends at a restaurant or out for drinks

- visit our disabled or elderly relatives and friends who crave our companionship

- wear a mask that conceals a warm smile

***

We are wired for connection—and yet, "flattening the curve" works against that natural wiring. The virus flourishes with connection, just as much—or even more—than we do.

Creative Prompts

When have **you** acutely experienced, deep in your spirit, the truth that: "We are wired for connection"? When was that moment and what happened? How did you, at a deep level, know this to be true?

Make a paper chain with strips of paper that are closed with tape/glue/staples. On each link, write the name of someone in your circle that you are linked with. Celebrate how you are wired for connection.

The Pandemic as magi—wisdom giver

What's your favorite movie of all time?

What makes it your favorite movie? What is the plot line? More specifically, what is the challenge that creates the plot line? And what must the hero(es) of the story learn or discover within themselves in order to successfully complete the plot line? For example, often in romantic comedies, the hero must learn to be vulnerable to let the other person in, or to let themselves be seen. In superhero dramas, the superhero discovers that despite a concerns or sliver of doubt/weakness, he really can find it within him to prevail if he just digs to a deeper space within him that he has never yet accessed.

Think back in your life to the time when you experienced the greatest growth. When you learned something new, developed capacity you didn't know you had, or made a discovery about yourself or the world that changed your perspective.

Go ahead. Think a minute…

What was it? It was a time of challenge wasn't it? It might have been a challenge you took on that entailed struggle—like signing up for a marathon and training to get ready or going to school to get a degree. It might have been a time of darkness that was thrust upon you, like a divorce or job loss, that felt achingly painful, but you had no choice but to figure a way out slowly.

Barbara Brown Taylor, who speaks of times of darkness in our lives in ways that utterly fascinate me says this:

> *I let this sink in: new life starts in the dark. Whether it is a seed in the ground, a baby in the*

womb, or Jesus in the tomb, it starts in the dark.[14]

Wouldn't it be great if growth came with a side of onion rings after a walk on the beach? Gosh, I wish it didn't have to be that so much of my growth and learning has come out of darkness. I truly do. And partly for myself—but partly because if it is true for me, it must also be true for you.

Please understand that I do not **welcome** darkness in my life. I don't enjoy it. I don't even want it. I can't say that I'm thankful for the darkness itself—but I am grateful for the learning and growing that happened during times of darkness.

When I gave birth to twin sons who were stillborn, it was brutal. I thought I might go crazy with grief—loss, longing and feeling utterly and completely lost—all of it. The darkness that ensued threatened to drown me. I could go on for pages about how grief hijacked my life. For a long time, it didn't feel like any growth—it only felt like pain. There was no beauty in anything for me. However, from the vantage point of time, I can see how I became a different person because of how I experienced loss—more tender and compassionate. The loss has shaped the way I do therapy and has, therefore, influenced thousands of lives. I learned so much about suffering and strength and resilience—so much about myself and the world. But this is truth: If I could give all the learning back in exchange to being given the opportunity to raise Branden and Matthew—I'd do it in a heartbeat.

Times of struggle and loss are just *hard* when you're in the middle of it. If someone says, "This is a wonderful opportunity to learn and grow," right after your spouse dies or your son overdoses or you get laid off from your dream job, and you don't tell them you don't want to hear it, well, *I'll do it for you.* For some of you, COVID-19 as a wisdom teacher isn't possible when you're in the middle of tremendous sorrow—you can leave these chapters now and return to them in years to come. Others of us may already be noticing shifts within ourselves that are useful discoveries.

Creative Prompts

Think back to a time of struggle in your life.

---

[14] Taylor, Barbara Brown. *Learning to Walk in the Dark: Because God Often Shows up at Night.* Canterbury Press, 2015.

- What personal growth emerged from that time?

- What did you learn about the world?

- What did you discover that helped you be a better and stronger version of yourself?

Bring to mind someone whom you admire that has experienced considerable adversity in their life. You watch them and see that they have come out better, not bitter. They have weathered significant storms and can still enjoy the sunshine of life. Have a conversation with them about their resilience and growth. Write/draw/sing about what you learn.

Composting heartbreak

A couple of years ago, I was eating a team meal with my son's university team when they came to town for a mid-season match—exactly like the one I described in the earlier chapter, "The last normal day". I was visiting with his coach. This team had the number 1 ranking across the country the whole season thus far. The team was racking up enormous numbers of wins and was heading towards another championship. They were flying high with all the success on the court.

As part of the friendly chit-chat that happens over pasta and salad, I asked him about the season, and how he felt going into the second half of the season. I wondered aloud about his perceptions of the likelihood that the team would get the gold medal.

He told me something interesting. The coach said that he knew his team was excelling, but he wasn't sure that they had what it took to take them down the home stretch.

Coach had concern the team hadn't had to face enough adversity this year.

He reflected on other years where there had been significant challenges or crises with injuries or other difficulties.

He said that facing challenges together creates growth and enhances a sense of *team*. Overcoming difficulties is one way a team powerfully coalesces. When a team has faced adversity, they struggle together—unite at a deeper level. This, in turn, enhances performance.

It is something I've mulled about in my head in the years since: A coach appreciating the fruit of a team struggling with hardship.

The alchemy of tribulation is important in a team's success.

Hard times make the team stronger, better.

Turns out, that though this team sailed through that season, they lost in the finals.

***

Jim and I were part of an article a few years ago in the Globe and Mail, a national Canadian newspaper. Zosia Bielski, a writer from the Globe, contacted me after reading an article I wrote, Visiting My Husband's Wife's Grave[15] on our website, ConexusCounselling.ca[16]. She wanted to write about finding love quite soon after loss of a spouse that was compassionate and understanding.

Finding love "quickly" after a spouse dies is a *deeply personal* topic for me. This could not remain an interview that focused on my professional expertise. She asked specific details that felt deeply personal—even asking how much time had passed between my Jim's wife's death and our marriage. It felt hugely vulnerably—it opened us up to the judgement of an entire country to say that it was 13 months. Then she asked for a wedding photo of the two of us for the article.

I really needed to think.

I talked about it with Jim. We talked about the exposure of sending a picture to be used in an article about how harshly people can judge, *Too soon? Why we harshly judge the widowed when they find new love[17].*

To put a wedding pic on an article like this seemed like we were setting ourselves up to be skewered by criticism. It's safer in the shadows. To be out front invites judgement to have people see us as we share of some tender experiences.

Vulnerable, for sure.

---

[15] Klassen, Carolyn. "Visiting My Husband's Wife's Grave - Conexus Counselling - Winnipeg Manitoba." *Conexus Counselling,* 27 Mar. 2019, conexuscounselling.ca/2015/10/09/visiting-my-husbands-wifes-grave/.

[16] Look for a treasure trove of resources on our website: "Home - Conexus Counselling - Winnipeg Manitoba." *Conexus Counselling,* conexuscounselling.ca/

[17] Bielski, Zosia. "Too Soon? Why We Harshly Judge the Widowed When They Find New Love." *The Globe and Mail,* The Globe and Mail, 15 Jan. 2018, www.theglobeandmail.com/life/relationships/too-soon-why-we-harshly-judge-the-widowed-when-they-find-newlove/article37607669/.

But we the question we came around to was this:

"What if some good could come out of this pain?"

One of my favorite shows, This is Us, has a line that has threaded throughout several episodes:

> *Sometimes life is about taking the sourest lemons life has to offer and making something resembling lemonade.*[18]

In the first episode the obstetrician, Dr. Katowski, played by Gerald McRaney, approaches Jack, a brand-new dad. His wife just had triplets—and one died during birth. While seeking to comfort him at the death of his child, Dr. Katowski expresses the lemonade idea. He shares his own experience of infant loss—and how that impacted his choice of career. An infant has been abandoned and is lying in the hospital nursery needing a home—and Jack and his wife will adopt this infant into their family.

We discover in a later episode that the obstetrician had intended to end his own life earlier that day because he didn't feel like was worth living after his wife died. His plan for suicide had been interrupted by a call from the hospital to deliver the triplets. He discovers he is able to use the depth of his grief to give hope to a heartbroken dad—because he understands the heartbreak of death. He rediscovers purpose and meaning through this family and goes on to live many more years. The conversation about lemonade to a broken-hearted dad was itself lemonade to a broken-hearted widower.

***

Going through painful life experiences hurts like heck.

Why wouldn't we want to use every opportunity to ***turn the painful crap of our lives into something resembling rich compost?*** Compost provides a nutrient rich medium that enhances growth.

We *can't* **undo** the hurt. We *can't* **stop** painful and unfair experiences in lives.

We *can* **compost** the heartbreak. We *can* **make** it into something that doesn't have to stay ugly and soul destroying—it becomes life-giving and redemptive.

Turning the pain into something life-giving just seems redemptive.

---

[18] Ficarra, Glenn and John Requa, directors. *This Is Us - Lemonade Scene.* 9 Aug. 2019, https://youtu.be/ZCI9Xr0bdXQ.

Creative Prompts

Look around—in the news and in your life. Now and in the past. Find examples of people who have composted the painful crap of their lives into fertile soil that created meaningful growth. What got composted? What grew out of it? Perhaps draw a plant growing from the crappy compost turned fertile soil. Label the compost with the pain. Name each leaf with a person's name or a quality of growth that arose out of the compost.

Are there some small ways in which you have already composted your corona-crap? Perhaps using the time at home to make a sign to put in your window? Ordered in food from a local restaurant to give them support? Journal about how you have sought to make a difference—done good in ways that wouldn't have been possible without.

Redemptive suffering

D r. Viktor Frankl was a psychiatrist, a guy who hung out with Sigmund Freud. He felt strongly that it was possible to find redemption in all suffering. Frankl felt we could find redemption in all suffering.

And right about now, as you are sitting at home for yet another week without a job or a hope of one, or grieving the loss of a neighbor from COVID-19, or wondering if going grocery shopping could lead to virus spread to your elderly mother who has cancer, you're thinking, "Wait. Huh? Like, seriously?"

Isn't suffering just plain suffering?

Let me say: Frankl earned the right to speak about redemptive suffering. He was Jewish physician living in Europe before and during World War II. He lost his wife, mother and brother to the horrific actions of the Nazis. He himself spent time in concentration camps. It was in those camps that he encouraged men not to despair and end their life with suicide when everything seemed hopeless and desperately bleak. He encouraged the men to only die at the hands of the Nazis. If they died by murder rather than suicide, they would actively be part of the throng that denounced the atrocities of the Nazis to show the world what was happening.

Victor Frankl said this:

In some ways, suffering ceases to be suffering at the moment it finds a meaning, such as the meaning of a sacrifice.[19]

---

[19] Frankl, Viktor E., and Ilse Lasch. *Mans Search for Meaning: an Introduction to Logotherapy: a Newly Rev. and Enl., Ed. of From Death-Camp to Existentalism.* Washington Square Press, 1962.

There could be a danger in using meaning to short circuit the path out of suffering. I watched an interview with a gentleman whose wife and several of his children perished in a house fire, and he spoke about purpose and meaning the day after their deaths. It rang hollow.

Likely you also know someone that feels like they have failed at suffering because they aren't somehow finding purpose and value in meaning—in fact, they can't fathom a purpose to their suffering. Often, we can't in the middle of it. Meaning isn't intended to launch us on a fast track out of the pain of suffering—though some have tried it, generally unsuccessfully.

However, knowing that meaning could, at some point, emerge out of suffering can change one's perspective.

***

In 2005, I found myself in the midst of despair. I was watching my life as I had known it crumble both *behind my back* and *before my eyes*.

I silently bore witness to my marriage dissolving. It sucks to watch your life fall apart over several months, desperate to do anything to save it–but seeing that any attempt to rescue it only sped up the pace of the disintegration.

Here I was, a marriage therapist, helpless to do anything to save her own. Yes, ouch. Yikes. ohmigosh…no, no, no, no. But yes–and helplessly so.

Short of *changing my gender*, there was absolutely nothing to be done. Nothing.

And I was *devastated*.

A decade later, I went to a writing workshop that challenged me to find the redemptive aspects to this time. I wrote about how, because of the death of my marriage, Bergen and Associates Counselling (now Conexus Counselling) developed.

Bergen and Associates Counselling was *never* planned.

I *never intended it to happen.*

Bergen and Associates Counselling was *born out of necessity*–as a single mom I needed to provide for my children while also being present with them before and after school–and everyone knows most couple therapists are busiest in the evening. I wanted to work outside the house during school hours only. I engaged therapists to work under contract for me, to take the clients that could only come on weekends and evenings when I would be at home with my children. I could do the administration for this after the children went to bed. I was home when they went to school, and home when they came home. And while it was exhausting to work late at night most evenings, I could buy the groceries and pay the mortgage. I started a blog to promote the practice—it is widely read. I could never have written the way I did if I had been married. The solitude gave me the space to write. The blog led to speaking, and speaking led to a TEDx talk and to writing—including this little guided journal book.

This book now wouldn't be in your hands if my marriage hadn't died then.

I love our clinic. We offer quality therapy using state of the art programs that are proven to improve results. We have four clinic spaces in two different locations, offering services 7 days/week. We are told that we have a solid reputation in the community. Hundreds of people are impacted by the sessions and services we offer. Every. single. week.

We receive cards and letters from folks who tell us their marriages are stronger, their kids are healthier, their lives are more fulfilling, their depression has lifted, and their anxiety is no longer crippling because of the work that has happened within our walls. People's lives are changed because this group therapy practice exists.

Something remarkably special was created to help the people who walk through our doors. It never would have happened if I wasn't scrambling to survive.

I have discovered parts of myself I never knew existed. I am now invited into cool projects because others believe me capable. Who knew? I didn't! I am now aware I have strength to push through difficult times that I couldn't have known about without this difficult time. I learned that I can be terrified and still get something done. I was pushed to think through issues of suffering and loneliness in ways that have carved me gentler. I'm more compassionate and understanding.

I think I'm a better therapist because my marriage ended. Gail Caldwell writes:

> *I know now we never get over great losses; we absorb them, and they carve us in different, often kinder creatures.*[20]

***

I know what it's like to want something–like staying married–so bad I could hardly breathe. And then I had to still somehow catch a breath, even though I was powerless to hold onto my marriage.

I know the physical pain borne by those in grief. There is a physical ache that bears heavy and constant for a long time. The fatigue that happens with grief and loneliness

---

[20] Caldwell, Gail. *Lets Take the Long Way Home: a Memoir of Friendship*. Random House, 2011.

that cannot be shook–it's exhausting to feel you've lost a part of you, and to figure out how to live when an essential part of you is gone.

I know what it is like to have the breath knocked out of you and the struggle to inhale seems too much. Yes, been there. Done that. Bought the T-shirt. And wore it night after night trying desperately and in vain to have it keep me warm.

The ripple effects of the end of my marriage continued. My sons attended a different high school than they would have otherwise attended because of the curve ball our lives took after I became a single mom. They have both made deep, significant lifelong connections that will alter the course of their lives, in life-changing ways. One found his life partner at that school. One had a sports scholarship to university after excelling at volleyball because of the quality coaching available at that school.

***

The death of my marriage was painful–I was lonely, sad, disillusioned and broken–for a long time. It is something I ***never*** wanted to have happen.

But it did. It ended, without my having any input into the whole thing. I didn't get to decide. I wouldn't have been able to predict what would happen. Life seemed bleak and impossible, for a long time.

Beauty can rise out of *ashes*.

And the gorgeousness of my life now sometimes takes my breath away.

Creative Prompts:

Think back to a time of significant struggle in your life. Remember and describe the pain, the loss, and the struggle. Don't sugar-coat the hard stuff to rush to the good stuff. Remember the agony that was a part of the initial experience and the time after in full color. (Note: for those of you with past trauma history, and who are aware that it would be retraumatizing to explore the pain, please don't do this. Please don't set yourself up to be triggered by this. You may choose to remember a time of struggle that feels manageable for this exercise, or not do this one at all. Please take care of you.)

Now look at the experience in a redemptively. What happened after that could only have happened because of the suffering? What sort of growth happened? What relationships developed? How were you changed? How did you become differently equipped as a human being? How were others impacted?

Write a letter to those that follow you in your future. What would you want them to know about life that you could only know because of your grueling experience?

Contemplate the reality that my story of redemptive suffering is long after my marriage ended in 2005. It may be a long time before you are able to know how beauty may rise out of the ashes of the COVID-19 pandemic. What is it like to know that we are planting seeds of the idea of redemptive suffering that may not be harvested for many years? Can you be patient with yourself? What does it look like to leave this part of your story unfinished until years of life unfold?

Gratitude

A few days ago, I wrote this on our Facebook page:

Let's celebrate! You made it through another day.

Another day of too much nothing when minutes drag like hours and it seems like it might be Tuesday or Sunday or 4 pm when it's only noon.

Another day of parenting children whose nervous systems are wrung tight by too many screens and not enough friends.

Another day of aching to see a vulnerable family member who you must stay away from as an act of caring—which still seems so very, very wrong.

Another day of spending too many hours with the same people who are in your space when you're an introvert.

Another day of spending too many hours at home with hardly any people when you're an extrovert and these people just won't cooperate with your need for saying all the WORDS!

Another day of beating yourself up for being too much "this" or not enough "that".

*Another day when you weren't sure if you could make it through—**but you did**.*

Celebrate! Here's a virtual fist bump to you!

Pass this on to someone who you want to virtual fist bump. We will make it through this together!

***

This pandemic has been a profound reminder for me to celebrate the small stuff; to focus on the little things and be amazed by them. Yes, making it through one more day of stay-at-home orders is something to be grateful for! Something to honor and acknowledge as significant.

And when something is worth celebrating, it's something for which to be grateful.

**

I've promoted gratitude as a helpful resource for mental health for a long time. The research on gratitude[21] as a conduit to experience joy beyond immediate circumstances is compelling. Gratitude as a disciplined practice makes a difference.

***

There are a number of ways I believe gratitude is a factor in these days of COVID-19.

1. Gratitude for things I used to take for granted. I used to live my life without gratitude for all sorts of things that I now don't have:

   - I enjoyed being able to pop into the grocery store to get a carton of milk on my way home, and then pop in later to get something for tomorrow's supper. Easy convenience.

   - I liked being able to hug my co-workers when they told me a story of something hard on the weekend.

   - It was a gift to chat with other parents on the sidelines of my son's games.

   - The richness of sitting down with a friend over coffee at Starbucks is absolutely wonderful

   - I love going out to a restaurant with my friend Judy. She picks a local place that has a rising reputation and we order what the server says is his/her favorite items on the menu. We howl with laughter at some points of the meal and pass the tissues for weeping at other points.

When I again have opportunity to resume these activities, I will be grateful for them with a sweetness I couldn't have had before this pandemic. Sometimes, we forget how beautiful the seemingly insignificant things are until we don't have them. The moments of face to face connection, the touches between friends of physical affection will be exquisite to feel again. Right now, I'm working to remind myself of all that I will be grateful for

---

[21] Emmons, Robert, et al. "Why Gratitude Is Good." *Greater Good*, 16 Nov. 2010, greatergood.berkeley.edu/article/item/why_gratitude_is_good.

when I can again do those things.

    2.   Gratitude for the kindness in now

During this time of COVID-19 when there is illness and restrictions, one thing that keep me going is the kindness all around me. I'm so grateful for the creativity and the whimsy that has emerged as people are good to each other

- The neighbor next door moved from France to play soccer here brings over an apple pie his wife has made for us. He doesn't speak English; I don't speak French. But we pantomime and use very basic words to check on the health of each other's family.

- I go for a walk around the neighborhood and I see signs of encouragement in the windows for us as well as gratitude for the front-line workers

- Every day there is a new video[22] online of a virtual group who have figured out how to bless us with a song

- Our office manager's husband works at a drugstore and the local pita restaurant brought supper to the entire staff to thank them for their service.

- The friend from Jim's widower's club had his wedding during the pandemic. They had 9 people in the church, and only about 25 cars allowed with social distancing in the parking lot. They invited Jim and I to be a part of the parking lot celebration after they found out how meaningful their wedding was to me. April 11 will now be known as the day of the wedding that defied the virus[23], rather than the anniversary of my date of marital separation.

    3.   Gratitude for the inspiration of front-line workers. I am inspired by front-line workers who go into impossible situations in the Intensive Care Unit. Some of them have travelled across the country to help out in hotspots like New York, risking exposure. Others self-quarantine away from their families to do the work and keep their children safe. While we do our part by staying

---

[22] I just can't get enough of this one: "Lean on Me - ArtistsCAN (Official Video)." ArtistsCANVEVO, 26 Apr. 2020, Lean on Me - ArtistsCAN (Official Video).

[23] Klassen, Carolyn. "April 11, 2.0 A Wedding in the Time of COVID-19 - Conexus Counselling - Winnipeg Manitoba." *Conexus Counselling*, 28 Apr. 2020, conexuscounselling.ca/2020/04/12/a-wedding-in-the-time-of-covid-19/.

at home, they do their part by walking towards the virus to save lives. They speak up about the need for more protective equipment and dire conditions, even while online trolls criticize and disbelieve. Watching them do their work inspires me to be a better person.

There is so much tragedy in the time of pandemic. However, daily, my heart is pulled to gratitude. It has often been amid my greatest suffering that the small acts of kindness have sustained me. I believe it is a beautiful thing to be grateful—and where possible, to express that gratitude.

Creative Prompts:

Craft a list of all the pre-COVID-19 things about which you now can only reminisce. What of those things were you grateful for? What will you most appreciate if you can return to them?

What are special COVID-19 moments that you have experienced, where someone troubled themselves to extend a kindness to you? Even a friendly look above the mask at the checkout is a gift! Perhaps create this list in a manner that allows you to add it as the days go on.

What are stories you've seen or heard that inspire gratitude in you?

During this time of pandemic, start a practice of gratitude. Something you do daily to be mindfully and deliberately grateful. Ideas:

- Write 5 things every evening of moments of gratitude during the day in this journal. Do this daily.

- Have a prayer of thanksgiving at every breakfast

- Have each member of the family express a gratitude every day at suppertime

- Snap a photo with your phone of something that strikes you as something to be grateful for that day. Gather those into a separate folder on your computer. At some point, publish them into a coffee table book as a creative memory.

- Get a recipe box and put 365 recipe cards on it. On the first one, put today's date on it and list one thing you are grateful for just underneath the date. Put it at the back of the recipe box behind all the other cards. Do the same thing tomorrow. A year from now, the card with today's date will have made its way to the front where you can see what you wrote a year ago, and add another item of gratitude to be seen the following year.

- Draw a quick image of something to be grateful for in an art journal book a couple of times a week. On the weekends, or when you have time, you can take time to draw borders, add color or words.

Notice what happens to your spirit as you develop and then maintain a practice of gratitude. As you are mindful, create something that acknowledges what you discover.

Send a note by text, email or snail mail to someone letting them know how much you appreciate them or what they did. You will make their day!

Existential discovery

We won't be able to go back to life as we know it. Even if they discover how to conquer this pandemic tomorrow, there's no going back:

- So many have passed away. The end of the pandemic will not bring them back.

- Many will be recovering from the lingering effects of the virus after they have officially "recovered". They are weak, short of breath easily, struggling with "COVID brain fog".

- We have learned information about broken systems that we best not forget. For example, personal care home staff haven't been given the respect they are due and that can't continue.

- We have discovered that some of us can work just fine from home. Board meetings with people across the world can happen using video meetings rather than flying to the same location at much time and significant expense.

- Some kids have discovered they learn better from home, or even if they don't learn better from home, they have learned more about their best learning styles. Some of them have learned their worst learning styles.

- We have discovered clearer skies, fish can now be seen in the canals of Venice, goats in the city streets and turtles scuttling barrier free to the ocean after hatching. The world has taken in a breath of clean fresh air and it has exhaled with new life.

I don't think anybody really knows what the world will look like after COVID-19 stops being a threat.

No doubt there will be hardship as we figure out how to pay for all the subsidies given out these last months. People will be applying for work because their jobs no longer exist. Others will look at what used to be their restaurant or business front—something they have built over a lifetime has gone *belly up*. They will have to figure out how to move forward without the passion they poured themselves into for years.

It will be difficult and painful for so many, in so many ways.

Nothing can put a silver lining on this loss in ways that make it worth it.

Nothing.

However, I remain hopeful.

We have done so much together, apart. We have recognized the value of human connection. Strangers have looked each other in the eye and nodded gestures of greeting. I can see eyes crinkling in a friendly smile even if a mask covers the toothy grin. Many have ordered takeout as a discipline to ensure cooks have jobs, and delivery people have meals to deliver.

I have learned about the value of a sustained slower pace of life. I have loved not scrambling to get everyone fed before a flurry of evening activities. I take inordinate pleasure in drinking morning coffee while quietly sitting and watching the birds come and go from the bird feeder in the back yard.

I don't want to go back to the hustle bustle scramble of pre-pandemic life. I've learned something from the rhythms of stay-at-home life that I don't want to lose. I don't know what my life will look like after the pandemic, but I'm trying to be mindful of how I am hoping it won't be the same.

Art is inspiring me to look for an existential meaning in this pandemic. It is not—cannot—at all be fully formed and thought out now, but I am inspired to hold space for what this time might teach us as individuals and as a world community.

The Praise Song for the Pandemic[24] by Christine Valtner Paintner is one such poem. Please go watch and listen, right now! It includes this line:

When this has passed may we say that love spread more quickly than any virus ever could,

May we say this was not just an ending but also a place to begin.

---

[24] Paintner, Christine Valters. "Praise Song for the Pandemic." *Vimeo*, 15 May 2020, vimeo.com/404108104.

The Great Realisation[25] is a beautiful poem by Tomos Robertson, crafted into video that addresses the possibility with childlike simplicity in the form of a bedtime story. This sweet piece of creativity warms me, thoroughly.

The virtual choirs, virtual orchestras, exercise classes and evening songfests from balconies, evening cheers for health care workers, and evening talk show hosts with their preschoolers crawling all over them all inspire us to show us that there is beauty amidst struggle and joy amidst pain.

Creativity is getting us through the pandemic, and it will get us out of the pandemic. Creativity is our path out of this era.

Creative prompts:

Sit quietly for some time in a favorite place with a favorite beverage with your favorite candle with your favorite music quiet in the background. Ask yourself, "What of this time do I want to take with me? What can this world learn because of this pandemic?" Listen for the quiet responses that might emerge.

Craft something to illustrate the answers. Write a poem. Sew a quilt. Make a collage from bits you cut out of magazines. Make a video. Come up with your own idea.

I'd love to see it. We all would. If you can, post it in some fashion and give it the hashtag: #MentionableisManageable. We will look for it.

---

25 "The Great Realisation." *The Great Realisation*, Tomos Robertson, 29 Apr. 2020, https://youtu.be/Nw5KQMXDiM4.

Grace

We don't talk much about "grace" in our world. I think that's unfortunate. I've been talking about it all the time in the last weeks. I'm convinced that it is grace for ourselves and each other that will get us through this pandemic. The pace of stay-at-home orders have many of us have time to look up and look around for where to extend grace to those who need it. The call of duty has people rise up to extend grace in the face of adversity in ways that seem both brave and sacred. Our breath is taken away by the many ways in which people show up to give pizzas to strangers, drop off groceries to the isolated, and honk and cheer as heroes pass by.

***

Grace came over in the form of my son's accounting teacher last week.

The teacher must have had to take off his halo when he put his bike helmet on to cycle over to our place to have a socially distant conversation with us.

I think we are all starting to realize that the lessons kids are learning about coping and struggle and grit and balance and relationship outweigh the objectives of Precalculus and Canadian History. These are also important, I recognize, but these are strange times, and these are not the lessons that students will remember. Learning book knowledge has taken a back seat to coping with life in our house in this season.

Mr. J. met us on the back deck to talk about the realities of how hard homeschooling is. He is an active guy that reminded us that all these hours in front of a screen are hard on everybody and make productive learning super difficult. He understood the struggles of a Junior Tribe Member trying to learn high school material under these circumstances. He was compassionate without being indulgent.

Our son is a super-bright guy, but, like most kids, he was not meant to learn alone in front of a screen. Our son said that his tears were about to start when we looked at the reality of how far behind he was in this course. Then they dried up when the teacher started talking solutions.

We clarified this young man is not cut out to be an accountant—balancing a corporate budget is not in his future. He has enough knowledge of spreadsheets from the first part of the year for the teacher to pivot and say: "Time for him to invest in a new type of learning—one that is actually best for this time."

This teacher recognized the assignment hole this boy of mine was in and presented a creative solution that is totally student centered. He offered a way out. And this way out encourages activity and kindness and fitness and growth. Unconventional but super helpful:

One hour of exercise, cooking, errands, housecleaning, helping a grandparent = one assignment.

Anything that makes his or somebody else's life better counts towards assignment completion.

Hearing this made my eyes teary. The way out was a way up for my boy.

The teacher extended an offer that might not make him better with the columns that calculate a tax rate, but did motivate him with behaviors that will get him (and his parents) through this pandemic. This act of compassion had him let go of assignments to embrace a meaningful life that he was struggling to figure how to grab. Mr. J. gave him the handle to hold.

This teacher chose to extend grace and kindness in a way that will change our boy. I know it already changed me.

***

Today I wish you Grace:

Grace to sustain you through yet another day, perhaps one of no human contact, alone in front of a screen. Grace to endure yet another day without embracing another human being even as your skin aches for touch.

Grace to sustain you through the tantrums of wired children who just want to have their friends over for a playdate and instead have to figure out math with a parent who doesn't understand the "new math". The math of your life doesn't add up because you are only one person and yet required to do more parenting and office work than you've got hours in the day.

Grace for yourself as you look in the mirror to see grey roots that scream for a hair stylist and yet will live to see another day—or week or month. For you who longs to do something normal like to see a movie or drive over to visit a friend on their couch.

Grace for you as you go to bed feeling the weight of all that you planned to do but got left undone amid the COVID-19 distress.

Grace for your spirit as you bear the uncertainty of yet another week of a pandemic you have never known before—and nobody else has either. No one can tell you how this will end, and that's hard.

***

We need radical grace for this time. It's hard to extend grace when people make changes that feel like they challenge the very corest of your core values. It's not easy being generous in your assumptions of others. It's vital to hold fast to believing that everyone is doing the best they know how in a time when "best" is often unclear.

We need to get through this together.

And for that—we will require grace.

The hard part of grace is extending it when the hand that reaches for it has not extended it first and may well not reciprocate. But we don't get out of harsh and ugly circumstances by returning hate with hate. Rather, we transform the world by grace.

***

Can I invite you to a posture of radical grace?

- Grace to be kind to others who make decisions so vastly different from yours

- Mercy to those who feel the desperation points in their lives at different places than yours

- Compassion for those who are much more cautious that you

- Kindness to those who take different risks than the ones you are taking

- Empathy for others, as they move forward during this pandemic, who think very differently than you

More than ever, I wish you peace and compassion for yourself and for others in the coming days.

Creative Prompts:

What stories of grace have you seen in the news, in your neighborhood?

In what ways have you experienced grace?

In what ways have you extended grace to others?

What does *radical* grace look like in your life? What is/are the barrier(s) in your life that make it a challenge to extend radical grace to yourself and others?

Epilogue

You might have asked while you worked through the chapters and the creative prompts: "Carolyn, do you journal? Do you believe in this stuff? Do you draw or paint or write poetry to work through your reactions to the pandemic this world finds itself in?"

Here's the thing: I'm struggling too. I have eaten more potato chips than is good for me—though at times, I have managed to have a little bowlful rather than the whole bag. I sleep with my phone on my nightstand and more often than is good for me, I look at the news before my feet have been on the floor in the morning. I have lost my temper with our son living at home and had unproductive days where I spent too many hours playing solitaire on a device. I'm struggling like everyone else and it shows.

And yes, I do journal and get creative: you're holding it in your hands.

Much of what I wrote in this little book is a compilation of thoughts I've had as I've gone through the days of pandemic living, just like everyone else. I've spent time listening to people as a therapist as they've spoken of their lives—their struggles, secrets and victories. I've had to prep for media interviews on living through COVID-19. I've prepared a workshop that I am delivering to interested groups online to help them cope with the pandemic called COVID-19: Miscreant, Monster and Magi. And all of it has prompted me to write. I create jpg posters on the computer with lines that I need to hear—knowing that if I find them important, it is likely others might find them helpful too. You can find them on our blog at ConexusCounselling.ca or on our Facebook page.

This book developed out of my desire to think through and process my own feelings and reactions to the COVID-19 pandemic and all the ways it is impacting our world.

This book is my own attempt, however imperfect, to work through the questions at the end of each chapter. And I believe that it has been helpful for me. I'm calmer after I write. I feel less "at odds" with myself and my family. I hope this book furthers your own painful and difficult journey through this pandemic.

I would love to hear about what you've written, see the paintings and drawings that emerge. I would love to discover the insights you have about yourself—and likely then discover a thing or two about my own experience at a deeper level because of it. Please post on Instagram or twitter with the hashtag: #MentionableisManageable,

***

My dream is that this time during COVID-19 not be a "pause" where we only wait it out to be able to continue to live our lives once we've got this beast licked. I'm not even sure it can be an option to put our lives on hold until COVID-19 is beat.

My intention is this: "If I've got to go through this pandemic—I don't have a choice—then I will not waste it. I will use this time of darkness to learn and grow and discover more about myself and the goodness of this world. I will conquer COVID-19 in my own life because I will not let it be solely destructive. I'm will use it for my own purposes." I realize that it is easy for me to say this because I have not lost a loved one from COVID-19. I haven't lost my job or my house. But there have been times when my children have died, or my husband has left—and one of the things that got me through the latter darkness was the idea that I would exploit tragedy for my purposes. I would let the pain teach me. I would let the darkness be dark and see what I could learn. I would see the pinpricks of light shining through the darkness with the kindness of others and appreciate them in a way I never could in full sunlight.

About the author

Carolyn Klassen has completed a Master of Arts degree in Marriage, Family, and Child Counselling in Fresno, California. She also has a degree in Occupational Therapy from the University of Manitoba, where she went on to teach students in therapeutic communication for many years.

She is a therapist and founder of Conexus Counselling in Winnipeg, Manitoba, Canada.

A Certified Daring Way Facilitator, she believes that fundamentally, all of us are wired for connection, and that meaningful relationships have tremendous healing power. Carolyn now speaks widely on topics of resilience and connection.

She has a 2018 TEDx Winnipeg talk, Learning from the sequoias: the value of interconnectedness. She is passionate about helping people improve their relationships with themselves and each other. She has written books, *Nice to a Fault: Redefining Kindness in Marriage, Thinking Therapy: No to Maybe* and *Is there still time to run?* and a weekly conversation with Hal Anderson on 680CJOB. She loves lattés, family suppers, busy bird feeders, sun porches, and watching her sons play sports.

Carolyn would be extremely grateful for you review with a comment on Amazon. You are invited to contact her at info@conexuscounselling.ca

9 781777 225629